unning
rn
chusetts

BEN KIMBALL

Trail Running Western Massachusetts

University Press of New England | Hanover and London

University Press of New England
www.upne.com
© 2015 University Press of New England
All rights reserved
Manufactured in the United States of America
Designed by Mindy Basinger Hill
Typeset in Quadraat

For permission to reproduce any of the material in this
book, contact Permissions, University Press of New England,
One Court Street, Suite 250, Lebanon NH 03766;
or visit www.upne.com

Library of Congress Cataloging-in-Publication Data

Kimball, Ben.
Trail running Western Massachusetts / Ben Kimball.
    pages   cm
ISBN 978-1-61168-786-6 (paper : alk. paper)—
ISBN 978-1-61168-787-3 (ebook)
1. Running—Massachusetts—Guidebooks.
2. Trails—Massachusetts—Guidebooks.
3. Massachusetts—Guidebooks. I. Title.
GV1061.22.M4K56 2015
796.4209744—dc23   2014042895

5 4 3 2 1

PAGE i Upper Loop Trail at Hopkins Memorial Forest in Williamstown.
PAGES ii–iii Running along the Jug End Loop Trail in Egremont.
PAGES x–xi Swooping singletrack trail at Robinson State Park.

All photos by Ben Kimball.

Contents

Acknowledgments

This guide could not have come together without the assistance of my incredibly supportive partner, Jennifer Garrett; she helped with everything, including GPS work, editing, and overall logistics. Also, she occasionally stashed delicious treats in my backpack. Others who provided invaluable advice, insight, and encouragement include Michael Menard, Jeff Hansen, Patrick Pezzati, Vanessa Holford Diana, Rob Higley, Donna Utakis, Steve Engle, Jen Grant, John Shaw, Nate Davis, Dave Stauffer, Frank Bock, Tom Davidson, Jesse Pion, John McCarthy, John Torrone, Ross Krause, Meghan Lynch, Ana Wolf, my mother Ellen Kappes, and the many adventurous runners of the 413. I'd also like to offer special thanks to Mark Ogilbee for his eagle-eyed and indispensable editorial efforts. Many guidebooks and maps proved useful for scouting and investigating trails, including ones published by New England Cartographics, Berkshire Natural Resources Council, The Trustees of Reservations, Appalachian Mountain Club, Massachusetts Department of Conservation and Recreation, and various municipalities. All trails profiled in this book were surveyed and mapped in person, however, and any errors are entirely the responsibility of the author. Finally, cheers to the many conservation organizations, land trusts, recreation departments, hiking clubs, mountain bike clubs, and volunteers who build and maintain the wonderful trails of western Massachusetts.

Site Locations

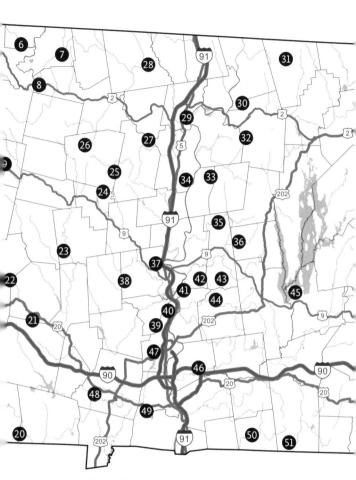

Trail Running
Western
Massachusetts

Trail at Buffum Falls Conservation Area in Pelham.

Introduction

Whether swiftly gliding through the woods, leaping over fallen logs, or soaring along scenic mountain ridges, trail runners always seem to be enjoying themselves. This is hardly surprising, since trail running combines the best aspects of many healthy and enjoyable activities. Among other things, it provides opportunities for achieving good fitness workouts, spending time outdoors exploring new terrain, and connecting to the natural landscape in a direct and personal way.

Compared to road running, trail running is generally a more tactile and engaging experience, constantly forcing you to be mindful and aware of the world around you. It also has less impact on the legs than running on pavement, and it strengthens different sets of muscles since it frequently requires the body to balance and stabilize itself. No special gear is needed, though trail running shoes can improve grip and comfort in various conditions such as mud, grass, and loose rocks, and either hand-held water bottles or backpack-like hydration packs are helpful on longer runs.

Hiking can be an integral part of trail running, especially on steep slopes, but there are a few key differences between the two activities. Clearly, you go lighter and faster when running, covering more miles in a shorter period of time and potentially moving more quickly past sights where you might otherwise linger longer. But you also feel the ground differently—you flow over it rather than just stepping on it—and you make crucial, split-second decisions about where to place your feet with each stride.

As evidenced by the emergence of many new trail races and series, and rising registration numbers at existing events, the sport has seen a huge surge in popularity in recent years. The appeal has clearly become apparent to the broader running community. While this guide features many sites for experienced runners seeking less-traveled but still interesting and fun trails further from the beaten path, it also aims to be inclusive, with a number of easily accessible sites for anyone looking for first-step exposure to trail running.

Western Massachusetts offers an incredible number of great trail running opportunities, from out-and-back runs on famous long-distance routes such as the Appalachian Trail and the Metacomet-Monadnock Trail, to little-known loops hidden away up in the hills. The intent of this book is to present a diverse selection of fun runs for you to enjoy. Geographically, it covers the area between the Quabbin Reservoir region in the east and upstate New York in the west, including the Pioneer Valley and Berkshire regions as well as portions of the Taconic Mountains. Elevations range from the lowlands of the Connecticut River and Housatonic River valleys to Massachusetts's highest point at the top of Mt. Greylock. The trails profiled also represent a range of difficulty levels and terrain types. There are options here for everyone. However, these are still only a sampling; there are many other great trails out there for you to discover and explore.

CONSERVATION With the rise of trail running's popularity has come an increased environmental impact on the beautiful trails and landscapes we all love to escape to. By promoting and practicing a low-impact mindset and suggesting best practices for treading lightly, we can try to preserve these treasured resources for our own future and for generations to come.

One easy principle is to simply avoid running on trails when they're vulnerable, particularly in the spring. As the snow melts from a long New England winter, everyone wants to get out and hit the trails. Unfortunately, this is when the impact from running can do the most damage. Ground saturated with snowmelt is soft and easily eroded, and formerly pleasant paths can quickly become ruts of exposed roots and rocks. Staying off the trails during the wettest spring weeks will help ensure that they remain in top shape for the rest of the year.

While it can be tempting to rocket down a steep pitch to get that feeling like you're flying, be aware that doing so has the potential to significantly speed up the process of erosion. The impact of each footfall is magnified when you're pounding downhill and sliding along loose rocks and gravel. It's always a good idea to avoid areas of loose or muddy soil in these cases. Even better, consider slowing down so that you tread more lightly on the land. It's also preferable to stick to the middle of existing trails—even if that means encountering a mud puddle or two—rather than going off to the side, which widens trails and hastens erosion unnecessarily. Lastly, never cut off a switchback in the trail; they're there specifically to prevent erosion.

Dispersing in both time and space is another way to reduce impact. If the majority of people frequent only the most popular sites, that resource can quickly be ruined and everyone's enjoyment lessened. Instead of always visiting a favorite trail, consider going to such places only on weekdays, when crowds are much smaller, and using your weekends to explore more remote, less-visited sites. Not only will you decrease use at the popular site, you may find greater solitude, have a more pleasant experience, and increase your appreciation for the natural diversity of the region.

Perhaps most importantly, you can get involved with conservation organizations that are committed to preserving and maintaining stewardship over natural areas and publicly accessible lands with trails. In western Massachusetts, there are many excellent land trusts you can support with financial pledges, service hours, or both. Furthermore, many of these groups host volunteer work days where you can help out and keep the trails fun to run.

ETIQUETTE Observing several basic rules of decorum will go a long way toward engendering goodwill with landowners and land managers and helping to ensure continued public access to a wide variety of trails. The more we present a positive image of runners as respectful and responsible users of trails, the better an experience everyone will have, and the more welcome we'll be in the future.

Encounters with other users are virtually guaranteed, even at the remotest of sites. Always be courteous of hikers, bikers, and other runners, making way whenever possible. Also, never underestimate the powerful goodwill that can be generated by a simple "hello" or friendly nod to a fellow trail user. If you encounter a motorized off-road vehicle (ORV) such as an all-terrain vehicle (ATV) or motorbike, you as a pedestrian have the right-of-way—technically. But step aside for them anyway, especially on any trails specifically designated for their use (a few are included in this book as part of larger circuits). You will likely hear them long before they see you anyway.

When following publicly accessible trails that cross private property, always respect the rights and desires of the landowners. Please obey all posted signs, especially "No Trespassing" signs, and never intentionally move or damage any on-site structures such as fences or gates.

Finally, bear in mind that while many trail networks (such as those in state parks and forests) were designed for a variety of recreational uses, others encourage as quiet and passive a use as possible. For example, running is specifically prohibited on trails at Mass Audubon properties; for that reason, none are included in this book. At properties where running is allowed but the primary purpose is conservation, please take extra care to not disturb wildlife, native vegetation, or other visitors who are there specifically to enjoy those things.

SAFETY While there are a number of factors to consider when planning a trail run, perhaps none is more important than hydration: you simply have to have enough water. There are dozens of handheld water bottles and hydration packs on the market in which you can carry water, sports drinks, whatever. Experiment with what works best for you. Just make sure you drink. For longer runs, consider stashing water bottles at accessible points along the route beforehand. Another option is to carry a second water bottle and deposit it at a spot you will be returning to later in your run—just make sure to remember *which* tree you hide it behind! One note of caution: never drink untreated water from an untested source.

Insects are probably the most common animals you'll encounter. Consider extra clothing or bug repellent to deter mosquitoes and blackflies, which can be maddening in large numbers, especially in the days following summer rainstorms. Tick-checks are a must after any run through shrubby or grassy areas. Wasps, hornets, and yellow jackets may also be encountered. Your best defense against them is to be on the lookout for nests, but should you accidentally stir some up or find yourself getting stung, just do what comes naturally: run away as fast as you can.

Encounters with large mammals are rare, but you may see deer, black bears, or moose. A black bear will typically run away should you happen upon one, but if it doesn't, back away and leave it be if possible, or make noise and try to look big if it appears threatening. In more remote areas, you might see a moose. These rarely charge, but it's best to stay out of their way and observe from a distance, just in case. Note that seasonal hunting is permitted on many of the properties profiled in this book. For up-to-date hunting season information, check with the Massachusetts Department of Fish & Game, and if you'll be running during an open season, wear bright orange clothing.

Naturally, trail runners must take care to avoid falls and physical injuries such as sprained ankles while out in the woods. Potential hazards to watch out for include wet rocks or ledges, slopes covered in loose gravel, and wet or slippery leaves. Practicing mindfulness and slowing your pace appropriately while making your way along a rough section of trail are necessary to ensure safe foot placement as you travel over the constantly changing terrain. Trail runners should also be aware of poison ivy; make sure you know what it looks like and where it tends to grow. Poison ivy often thrives in disturbed areas, and can be particularly dense right along the edges of roads, trails, and rivers, especially at lower elevations. Usually you can step over or pick your way through a patch along a trail, but a slight detour may be called for on occasion.

Always leave early enough in the day to make it back to the trailhead by nightfall, unless you plan to run with a headlamp. Also, check the weather forecast before heading out, particularly for remote sites or if taking trails that ascend to higher elevations. Prepare for the worst conditions possible and be willing to change your plans based on changes in the weather—even if it means cutting your run short. When it's wet and chilly out, be watchful for any early warning signs of hypothermia, such as cold feet and hands, pale skin, shivering, fatigue, or slurred speech. Hypothermia can be especially dangerous in temperatures just above freezing.

If there is a logbook or register at the trailhead, stop to sign in on the off chance an accident occurs and you need to be located. For the same reason, consider telling someone your intended route and an estimated return time.

TRAIL ACCESS All of the trails profiled in this guide are open to the public. Most are on public land or publicly accessible land, but occasional portions cross privately owned parcels. This is especially true of long-distance trails like the Metacomet-Monadnock (M-M) and Mahican-Mohawk (M/M) Trails. At present, it is not possible to travel end-to-end on these routes, as various portions have been closed (or are still incomplete, in the case of the latter). Only open portions were included at the time of this guide's writing, but users should be aware that trail closures or re-routings are possible at any time.

Note: In Massachusetts, the New England Trail (NET), a designated National Scenic Trail, follows the route of the M-M Trail, and along it NET logo markers can sometimes be found in addition to the M-M Trail's rectangular white blazes. For clarity, this guide refers only to the M-M Trail.

HOW TO USE THIS BOOK Every trail running route in this book has a chapter dedicated to it, and the chapters are organized both from west to east and north to south as numbered on the locator maps. Each site profile begins with quick-reference data that you can use to easily determine if that route is suitable for your running ambitions on a given day. This information includes:

Distance Total mileage of the suggested route (shortcuts and optional extensions to lengthen your run are usually detailed within the description of the main route).

Difficulty Rating Subjective categories of easy, moderate, and challenging, or a combination thereof.

Trail Style The shape the route traces on a map, including loop, lollipop loop (a loop with a "stick" portion), out-and-back, and figure-8 loop.

Trail Type The width and character of the trail itself; these include singletrack, doubletrack, and dirt road.

Town The nearest town or towns to help orient you to where the trail is located within Massachusetts.

This down-and-dirty data is followed by a general description of that chapter's route, highlighting some of the standout features you will encounter on the run. Next come directions to the trailhead from the nearest town or major highway; often directions are given from more than one direction.

The bulk of each chapter is given over to detailed, usually turn-by-turn trail descriptions on the route itself that—along with a judicious use of the maps contained in this book—should get you from start to finish without making a wrong turn or becoming mystifyingly lost in the wilderness. This section also often includes optional trims for shortening a given run if you don't want to tackle the entire trail that day or—alternatively—optional extensions for extending the run, sometimes by a significant distance. Occasionally, alternate options detail adjoining or adjacent routes that offer other worthwhile treks beyond the suggested route.

Finally, each site profile highlights other nearby sites that are good for trail running (there's a lot more than 51!).

For each site profiled, instant access (QR) codes are provided to link you directly to enhanced digital maps (as pdf files) and color photos. Scan the QR code with your smartphone (you will need to download a free QR scanning app) or, if you're reading this as an ebook, touch the code, to be directed to a web page for that site. This will allow you to bring a detailed version of the site map with you on your phone. If you'd prefer to print out one of these enhanced maps, visit trailrunningsites.com and click the link for the site you're visiting.

Trail running uses some descriptive but uncommon lingo

with which general readers (and some runners) may not be familiar. The following frequently used terms appear throughout the profiles:

4-way intersection where two trails cross

Doubletrack a trail wide enough for two people side-by-side

Fork like a Y-junction, only with two of the trails tighter together

Lollipop loop when a loop route starts with an out-and-back "stick"

Runnable a (highly subjective) term indicating "not too steep or technical"

Singletrack a trail wide enough for one person

Slabbing ascending a hillside on a straight diagonal

Switchback where the trail changes direction in a tight S or Z shape on an ascent or descent

Technical a trail with more rocks and roots than dirt, often with steep pitches

T-junction when one trail ends at another that is perpendicular to it

Woods road/dirt road similar to doubletrack, but slightly wider

Y-junction a 3-way intersection where all three trails split away at roughly equal angles

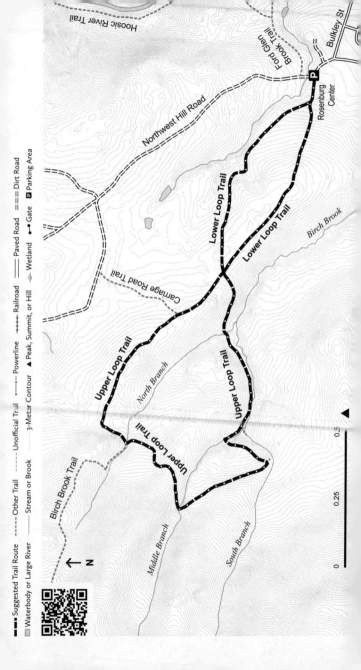

Legend:

- ▪▪▪ Suggested Trail Route
- ----- Other Trail
- ----- Unofficial Trail
- ++++ Powerline
- ━━━ Paved Road
- ═══ Dirt Road
- ⟿ Gate
- ━ Stream or Brook
- ▓ Waterbody or Large River
- ✦━ Railroad
- ─── 3-Meter Contour
- ▲ Peak, Summit, or Hill
- P Parking Area

Hoosic River Trail

Ford Glen Brook Trail

Bulkley St

Northwest Hill Road

Rosenburg Center

Lower Loop Trail

Lower Loop Trail

Birch Brook

Carriage Road Trail

Upper Loop Trail

Upper Loop Trail

Upper Loop Trail

North Branch

Birch Brook Trail

Middle Branch

South Branch

N ←

0   0.25   0.5

DISTANCE 4.5 Miles   **TOWN** Williamstown
DIFFICULTY RATING Easy/Moderate   **TRAIL STYLE** Loop/Out-and-Back
TRAIL TYPE Doubletrack/Dirt Road

In the far northwest corner of the state, Hopkins Memorial Forest features a network of mostly easy trails, offering great beginner routes for trail runners just starting out as well as nice tempo and hill workouts for more experienced runners. Owned and managed by Williams College, the property encompasses forestland that was once farmed and then later used as a research station by the US Forest Service. The figure-8 loop run described here utilizes several old roads. The main route is entirely doubletrack, and the optional extensions are singletrack. While never particularly difficult, this route includes a significant amount of elevation change, nudging the rating up to easy/moderate.

DIRECTIONS From the traffic circle junction of Rte. 7 and Rte. 2 in Williamstown, go west on Main Street. In 0.7 miles, turn right on Northwest Hill Road. In 0.5 miles, just past Bulkley Street, turn left into the dirt parking lot with a sign for Hopkins Forest Parking. There is space for about eight vehicles.

TRAIL Starting at the parking area, follow the straight gravel driveway west to the Rosenburg Center and Buxton Garden. At the building, bear right and follow the right fork of the Lower Loop Trail, also called the Carriage Road Trail and the Horse Trail. Ascending gradually along the old dirt road, the trail passes numerous scientific experiments, several interpretive signs, a catwalk in the trees, and a sugar shack. At about 1 mile from the start, you arrive at a 4-way intersection where there is a stone bench; this is the middle of the figure-8 loop.

From the junction, bear right on the right fork of the Upper Loop Trail. In 0.2 miles, the Carriage Road Trail veers off to the right (it reaches Northwest Hill Road in 0.4 miles), but stay straight on the Upper Loop Trail, which ascends gradually. The roadway becomes rougher, but the footing is still generally good. In 0.6 miles, the trail swings left (south), crosses below a steeper slope on the right, and at 0.7 miles you reach a signed junction with the Birch Brook Trail.

> *Optional Extension* To add an extra 3 miles to your run, take the Birch Brook Trail west for 1.5 miles up the eastern slope of the Taconic Range to the Taconic Crest Trail. This trail is narrower, rougher, and much steeper than the Upper and Lower Loop Trails. For an even longer extension, from the junction with the well-blazed Taconic Crest Trail just north of Jim Smith Hill, take a 1.2 mile-route south along the Taconic Ridge to Rte. 2 in Petersburg Pass, or a 1.5-mile route north past several scenic views and across two state lines to The Snow Hole, a deep crevice where snow and ice usually linger well into the summer.

From the junction with the Birch Brook Trail, go south on the Upper Loop Trail. The trail immediately crosses the North Branch of Birch Brook on a bridge, then gradually rises along the side of the slope. In about 0.4 miles, it crosses the Middle Branch of Birch Brook on a curving wooden bridge and makes a sharp left. This is the high point of the run. From here, the trail descends gently to the southeast for about 0.4 miles. Just before reaching the South Branch of Birch Brook, it curves left and drops to another crossing of the Middle Branch. Several short, unmarked side trails lead off to the right to nice views of cascades and small brook weirs along this stretch. Soon you arrive back at the 4-way intersection.

Bear right on the Lower Loop Trail. At first the trail descends very gradually along the crest of a ridge, then more steeply as it drops down the eastern end of the ridge. At 0.7 miles from the intersection it arrives back at the Rosenburg Center where you emerge into a clearing behind a barn. From here, it is about 0.1 miles back to the parking area.

Optional Extension From the parking area, you can add an easy extra 3 miles to your run by doing an out-and-back along Ford Glen Brook and the Hoosic River. From the parking lot, go left on the dirt Northwest Hill Road and cross Ford Glen Brook. In about 0.1 miles the trailhead is on the right. Follow the Ford Glen Brook Trail and gently descend 0.3 miles to a junction with the Hoosic River Trail. Go left and follow the trail for 1 mile to its end at Wire Bridge Farm.

NEARBY About one mile south, several trails lead west from the Flora Glen area toward loop options up in Taconic Trail State Park. A few more miles due south, a conservation property called Field Farm Preserve (owned by The Trustees of Reservations) features miles of trails through mown fields and adjacent forestland along with spectacular views of Mt. Greylock and streams that disappear underground.

DISTANCE 4 Miles   TOWN Williamstown
DIFFICULTY RATING Challenging
TRAIL STYLE Lollipop Loop   TRAIL TYPE Singletrack

Pine Cobble is a southern spur of Vermont's Green Mountains, towering high over the Hoosic River valley below. The views from the peak itself are magnificent, and the trail network on the mountain is well maintained and generally in very good condition. The hilly route described here utilizes the popular Pine Cobble Trail and a portion of the Appalachian Trail, as well as a less-traveled path called the Class of '98 Trail that takes a less direct route to the crest of the ridge.

DIRECTIONS From the junction of Rte. 2 and Rte. 7 in Williamstown, go 0.6 miles east on Rte. 2. Turn left on Cole Avenue and go 0.8 miles north, crossing both the Hoosic River and a set of railroad tracks. Turn right on North Hoosac Road. Go 0.4 miles east and then turn left on Pine Cobble Road. A parking area with space for about eight vehicles is located 0.2 miles up the hill on the left, and the trailhead is about 100 feet further up the road on the right. There is no parking directly in front of the trailhead.

TRAIL From the Pine Cobble Trail sign, the blue-blazed trail bears right and roughly parallels the road, climbing into the woods at a gentle grade. In about 0.5 miles, the grade steepens and the trail begins ascending a series of steep switchbacks on wooden steps. After the switchbacks, the trail levels out and crosses a nearly level bench. At 0.9 miles, it reaches a junction with the Class of '98 Trail.

Take a left on the Class of '98 Trail. Ignoring the numer-

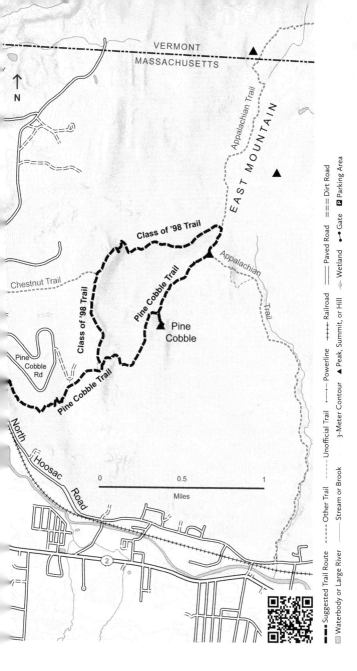

Looking south over Williamstown from Pine Cobble.

ous unmarked side paths leading off to the left, follow the trail north. For 0.5 miles, the trail stays just below a steep ledge on the right. It mostly follows a level contour, though there are a few rises and falls. In 0.6 miles you reach a junction with Chestnut Trail, which descends to the left (west). Bear right at this intersection and stay on the Class of '98 Trail.

Soon the trail begins to climb more steeply, and ascends the toughest part of the climb, a steep switchback across a forested talus slope. This section is marked with a subtle "Caution" sign, but the trail is well constructed and easy to follow. Above the switchback, the grade moderates and the trail begins a steady ascent heading east-northeast. At the crest of the ridge, go right (south) at a junction with the Appalachian Trail (AT).

Optional Extension To add an extra 2.5 miles to your run, go left on the AT for roughly 1.25 miles to the summit of East Mountain and the Vermont state line.

The trail quickly ascends to a sub-summit of East Mountain to the south, and another junction where the AT descends to the left. Stay straight on the Pine Cobble Trail at this junction. The trail briefly descends through a mostly open old burn site over a field of broken rocks, then enters the woods below. After descending at a moderate grade for 0.5 miles, the trail reaches a sign for Pine Cobble, where a 0.1-mile side trail leads right to several outcrops with stunning views of Williamstown, North Adams, Mt. Greylock, and the Taconic Range.

On the descent from Pine Cobble, the trail drops steeply over a very rocky section, passing a peculiar triple-trunked tree with a water-filled basin in its center. Soon the trail bears sharply right at a junction with an old trail, then passes a sign for the Pine Cobble Natural Area and reaches the junction with the Class of '98 Trail, closing the loop portion of the route. Follow the trail left back down to the trailhead.

NEARBY About 2 miles to the northwest at Mountain Meadow Preserve (a property owned by The Trustees of Reservations), trails cross into Vermont and offer incredible views from mowed paths through open pastures.

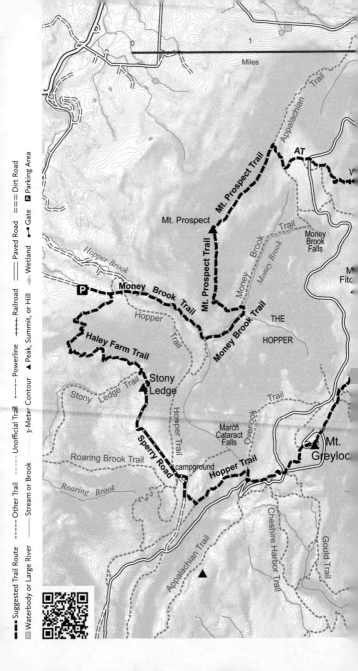

DISTANCE 13 Miles   **TOWNS** Williamstown/North Adams/Adams
DIFFICULTY RATING Challenging
TRAIL STYLE Loop   **TRAIL TYPE** Singletrack

If you've found most of the runs in this guide to be on the tame side: The Hopper awaits. The loop described here is arguably the most challenging in the list, primarily for the sheer steepness of the ascent. You will need to be in top shape to attempt this run. However, while it is very demanding, it is also very rewarding. The climb up Prospect Mountain notwithstanding, the trail is otherwise very runnable. The views from the top and other vantage points are amazing, the trails are mostly in good condition, and the final descent is extremely fun.

DIRECTIONS From Rte. 2 in Williamstown, go south on Rte. 43 for 2.5 miles. Turn left on Hopper Road and follow it south and east for 2 miles up to the large dirt parking lot at the end of the road.

TRAIL Starting at the parking area, take the Hopper Trail east over level ground through a line of trees between two fields. At the far end, pass the lower end of Haley Farm Trail on the right. Continue straight. In rapid succession, pass a junction with Hopper Brook Loop Trail on the left, a junction with Hopper Trail on the right (the trail becomes the Money Brook Trail here), and another junction with Hopper Brook Loop Trail on the left, staying straight at all junctions. At a small "dispersed camping" clearing, pass a short spur path to a spring on the right. Continue straight on Money Brook Trail. Descend gently to the brook and cross it on a wooden bridge.

Follow Money Brook Trail east along the north bank of the brook, then re-cross the brook at 1.2 miles from the parking area on another wooden bridge. Bear left at a junction with Cut Off Trail on the right and climb at a moderate grade on Money Brook Trail. In 0.5 miles, hop over two brooks (may be difficult in high water). Climb the slope on the other side to a junction and bear left on the Mt. Prospect Trail.

The Mt. Prospect Trail angles up the slope to the west, crossing a rocky slope and getting steeper as it goes. Then it veers hard right and climbs very steeply for about 0.5 miles straight up the spine of a narrow ridge. It reaches a nice vista ledge on the left, then climbs the rest of the way to the peak at a slightly less-steep grade. At the top (2,690 ft.), pass a large cairn on the left, then head north across the ridge. The trail reaches a vista overlooking Williamstown just before a junction with the Appalachian Trail (AT).

The next section mostly follows ridgeline to the summit of Mt. Greylock. Descend south on the AT to a 3-way junction. Stay left on the AT and follow it east past a trail to a parking lot on the right, cross over the paved auto road, and pass another trail to the parking lot on the right. Climb east at a steady grade for about 0.3 miles to the 2,951-ft. summit of Mt. Williams, then turn south and descend along the AT for 0.4 miles to a 4-way intersection with Bernard Farm Trail. Stay straight and follow the AT 1.4 miles south along the ridge crest, crossing over 3,110-ft. Mt. Fitch and arriving at a junction. Joining with the wide and open Thunderbolt Trail, take the AT 0.3 miles up to the 3,491-ft. summit of Mt. Greylock.

With several road crossings and sidewalk segments to follow, it's easy to get turned around at the top. Take care to stay heading south on the AT, but also make sure to take in the incredible views. After passing to the right of the war memorial tower and Bascom Lodge, the AT drops south into the woods. In 0.3 miles it crosses the road again and soon passes just to the left of a small pond. About 0.1 miles past the pond, leave the AT and turn right on the wide and rocky Hopper Trail (blue blazes).

Follow the Hopper Trail about a mile down to the west past several intersections, bearing right just before the road, left at the Overlook Trail, and right at Deer Hill Trail. Descend to the dirt Sperry Road and go right toward the campground. At the campground, a 100-yard detour to the right leads to a safe drinking water pump. Just past the start of the campground on Sperry Road, the Hopper Trail veers right into the woods.

Optional Trim to shorten the run slightly, you can take the Hopper Trail back to the parking area; it's about 2 miles of steady descending at a moderate grade.

Follow Sperry Road for 1 mile up to Stony Ledge where there is a spectacular northeastward view across The Hopper. From here, go west past the group camping site on Stony Ledge Trail and descend about 0.1 miles to a junction. Go right on Haley Farm Trail. The first mile descends somewhat steeply via multiple switchbacks to a small saddle where the trail swings right. From here, the final mile drops north via several switchbacks through a beautiful woodland. There are few rocks and the footing is very good. At the bottom, cross the west end of an open field and turn left at the intersection to return to the parking area.

NEARBY Many of the trails on the eastern side of Mt. Greylock, well-mapped and described elsewhere, are excellent for trail running. Notable highlights include Saddle Ball Mountain and Jones Nose, the Thunderbolt ski trail, and the Bellows Pipe, Bucket, Whitetail, Gould, and Cheshire Harbor Trails.

4 Savoy Mountain State Forest

DISTANCE 6 Miles **TOWN** Savoy/Florida
DIFFICULTY Rating Moderate/Challenging
TRAIL STYLE Loop **TRAIL TYPE** Singletrack/Doubletrack

The trails at Savoy Mountain State Forest allow for many different combinations of loops of varying lengths and difficulties. The route described here presents a sampling of the singletrack trails around North and South Ponds. Some sections are frequently wet and muddy, but the trails are generally excellent for running, and the scenery is very appealing. An added bonus right at the end of this run, at least in the summer, is a swim from the beach at the North Pond picnic area.

DIRECTIONS From Rte. 2 (the Mohawk Trail) between North Adams and Charlemont, go south on Central Shaft Road, staying right at the two junctions, for 3.5 miles to the paved parking lot at North Pond day-use area on the right. From Rte. 116 in Savoy, go 3 miles north on Center Road, then take a left and go 0.2 miles west on Adams Road. Take a right onto New State Road and go 1.5 miles north, then take a left on Burnett Road and go 0.5 miles west. Take a right onto North Florida Road and go 1.7 miles north to the spacious parking area on the left.

TRAIL Starting at the North Pond parking area, find the trailhead by heading past the bathrooms toward the pond and then turning left on the paved road that runs through the picnic area. Turn right and enter the woods on the singletrack North Pond Loop trail, blazed with blue triangles. The trail descends gently and then rises and falls across a few wet areas, reaching a 4-way intersection in 0.25 miles.

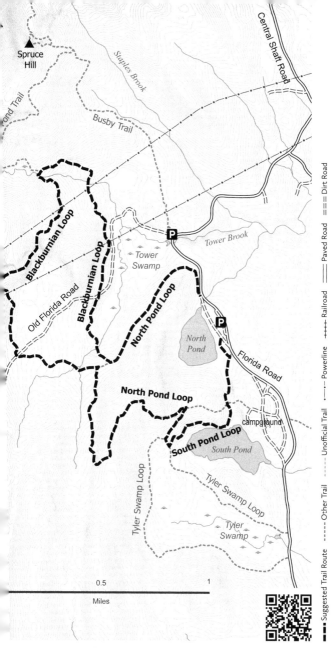

Spruce
Hill

Central Shaft Road

Staples Brook

Busby Trail

Blackburnian Loop

Blackburnian Loop

Tower Brook

Tower Swamp

Old Florida Road

North Pond Loop

North Pond

Florida Road

North Pond Loop

campground

South Pond Loop

South Pond

Tyler Swamp Loop

Tyler Swamp Loop

Tyler
Swamp

0.5   1

Miles

—●—● Suggested Trail Route   ----- Other Trail   ------ Unofficial Trail   —— Paved Road   === Dirt Road

—— Waterbody or Large River   —— Stream or Brook   ···· Powerline   +++ Railroad   3-Meter Contour   ▲ Peak, Summit, or Hill   ●— Gate   P Parking Area   ≈ Wetland

Optional Trim To shorten the run slightly, turn right on North Pond Loop trail and follow it 0.2 miles uphill to a 3-way junction, passing a glacial erratic boulder called Balancing Rock along the way. Then continue straight (west) up North Pond Loop trail.

Go straight (south) on South Pond Loop trail. In 0.1 miles, the trail arrives at a short spur down to the north shore of South Pond. From the shore, take the trail uphill and follow it 0.3 miles west to a 3-way junction. Here, Tyler Swamp trail goes left.

Optional Extension You can take Tyler Swamp trail and add an extra 2 miles to your run, but the portion of the loop on the south side of the swamp is extremely wet and overgrown, so you will need to be prepared to finish it with very wet (and likely muddy) shoes.

Take a right and very quickly reach a 3-way junction with the other end of Tyler Swamp Loop trail. Take another right and gently ascend 0.2 miles to a 3-way junction with North Pond Loop trail. Take a left on North Pond Loop trail. After climbing steadily to a ridge, the trail then drops down the other side over frequently wet ground and heads north to a junction with Blackburnian Loop trail. Take a left on Blackburnian Loop trail, which descends to a stream crossing and then climbs steadily to a junction with Old Florida Road, an eroded dirt roadway.

Optional Trim The run can be shortened by descending for 0.5 miles along Old Florida Road to a lower junction with the Blackburnian Loop trail, where you turn right. The rugged road is severely eroded but the many exposed rock ledges can be fun to descend.

After crossing Old Florida Road, the trail crosses a very wet area and then climbs to a powerline. Descend slightly along the powerline, then re-enter the woods on the far side and climb along a recently re-routed section of trail (portions of this section may be blazed with round, green and gold Mahican-

Mohawk Trail markers. In 0.6 miles, you cross another power-line. At 0.25 miles from the second powerline, the trail crosses a stream and reaches a 3-way junction with Lost Pond Trail.

> *Optional Extension* From here, it is possible to extend the run a few miles with a very challenging out-and-back climb along Lost Pond Trail and Busby Trail to the summit of Spruce Hill. Or you can create an alternate loop option by taking Lost Pond Trail to the summit and descending via Busby Trail to Central Shaft Road just north of the North Pond picnic area.

Turn right on the Blackburnian Loop trail and descend gently through a scenic woodland. The trail re-crosses the stream and then reaches and crosses a powerline. At a second powerline, you can see Old Florida Road running along the south side of an open wet area flooded by beavers. The trail re-enters the woods above the road, then climbs 0.2 miles to a junction with Old Florida Road. After crossing the road, the trail undulates 0.25 miles to a stream crossing, then climbs briefly to a 3-way junction with North Pond Loop trail. Go left here and follow North Pond Loop trail 0.8 miles down to Central Shaft Road. Take a right and follow the paved lane past a swimming beach to the picnic area and parking lot at North Pond.

NEARBY Several other trails at Savoy Mountain State Forest are worth exploring, including the Tannery Falls and Ross Brook Trails.

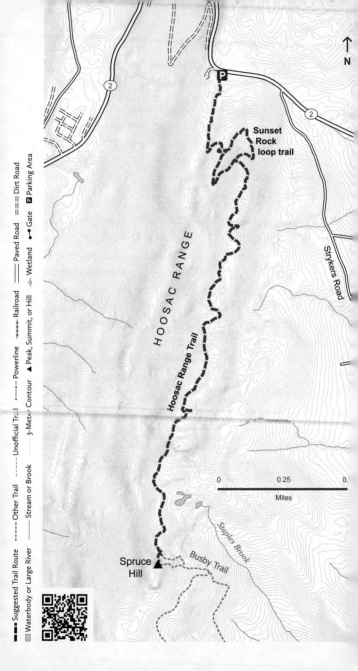

Sunset Rock
loop trail

HOOSAC RANGE

Hoosac Range Trail

Spruce Hill

Busby Trail

Staples Brook

Strykers Road

2

2

N

0   0.25   0.

Miles

Suggested Trail Route
Other Trail
Unofficial Trail
Railroad
Powerline
3-Meter Contour
Stream or Brook
Waterbody or Large River
Paved Road
Dirt Road
▲ Peak, Summit, or Hill
Gate
P Parking Area

DISTANCE 6 Miles   **TOWN** North Adams
DIFFICULTY RATING Moderate
TRAIL STYLE Out-and-Back   **TRAIL TYPE** Singletrack

The relatively new Hoosac Range Trail runs along the crest of a ridge for 2.8 miles from a parking area on Rte. 2 to the open summit of Spruce Hill in Savoy Mountain State Forest. Officially a link in the Mahican-Mohawk (M/M) Trail, this is an exceptionally well-constructed path. There are fun rises and falls along the way, but the footing is very good and for the most part it's very runnable. The grade along the mile-long climb up from the northern end is gradual enough to make for both a mostly runnable ascent and very pleasant descent on the way back. There are several trail junctions with side trails and spur paths, but all are well-marked and the main route is easy to follow. It is marked with rectangular white-and-red blazes, and sometimes with round, green-and-gold M/M Trail markers. Most of the land here is owned and managed by the Berkshire Natural Resources Council (BNRC) as the Hoosac Range Reserve.

DIRECTIONS The parking area for this trail, marked by a reddish BNRC welcome sign, is located along Rte. 2 (the Mohawk Trail) at a curve where the road crosses the height of land about 4 miles east of North Adams and 14 miles west of Charlemont.

TRAIL Starting at the parking area, the Hoosac Range Trail enters the woods behind an informational kiosk and begins climbing the slope to the south. The grade is gentle and the footing good. Very soon, you pass two man-made vernal pools on the left. In about 0.4 miles, you reach a junction with the

Sunset Rock loop trail. Go right here and ascend more steeply up the slope via a switchback for about 0.4 miles to an upper junction with the loop trail.

> *Optional Trim* If you reach Sunset Rock and are not feeling up for the full run, or time is tight, you can return via the other leg of the loop and make a 1.6-mile lollipop trip out of it.

From the upper junction, turn right and continue ascending to the south along the crest of the ridge. The trail meanders through rocky woodlands, and in May the understory is an endless carpet of trout lily wildflowers. The scraggly appearance of the forest is the result of the ridgeline's high elevation and extreme exposure; strong winter winds and heavy ice and snow regularly prune back upper tree branches. You pass a large vernal pool on the left, a large moss- and lichen-covered ledge on the right, and a few good-sized boulders along the way. Stone stair steps lead up and down several steep schist ledges. At 2.1 miles, a short spur path leads 0.1 miles left to a ledge with a limited view to the east.

Soon after the junction with the spur path, an unmarked old road leads off to the left. Stay on the main trail and keep heading south. When you cross an open utility line swath, you are nearly 2,000 feet directly above the Hoosac Tunnel, through which an active railroad still runs. At 2.7 miles, you arrive at a junction with the summit loop trail. Go right here and climb up the grassy ledge to a semi-open rocky crag just before the top. There are several nice views here, but keep going another 0.1 miles south. From the open rocky ledge, there is a spectacular 180-degree view southwest across the Hoosic River Valley and the town of Adams to the eastern slopes of Mt. Greylock.

It is possible to descend Spruce Hill via the blue-blazed Busby Trail to Savoy Mountain State Forest, and you could arrange a car spot at the base of that trail to make a very nice 4-mile point-to-point run; otherwise, return back the way you came along the Hoosac Range Trail. On your return trip, take a right when you reach the junction with the Sunset Rock Trail and go east about 100 feet to a sweeping, northwest-facing vista. Continue about 0.4 miles, first heading east and then veering left down the slope, to the junction with the main trail below. Then follow the M/M Trail north about 0.4 miles back down to the parking area.

NEARBY Across the Hoosic River valley to the west, the Bellows Pipe Trail runs at a gentle to moderate grade for 2.2 miles from a trailhead along Notch Road through a ravine between Mt. Greylock and a subsidiary peak called Ragged Mountain, with a steeper, 0.4-mile spur trail to a vista near the top of Ragged Mountain at the southern end.

DISTANCE 4 Miles   **TOWN** Williamstown
DIFFICULTY RATING Challenging
TRAIL STYLE Lollipop Loop   **TRAIL TYPE** Singletrack

It's easy to feel a sense of peaceful remoteness when running among the mountains, streams, and old trees of Monroe State Forest. The lollipop route described here generally follows the course of a popular trail race held at the site in the fall, with the addition of a short spur to a scenic vista at Raycroft Lookout on Hunt Hill. With steep climbs, occasionally rough footing, and a significant stream crossing where a bridge was washed out, this run is probably not for beginners, but experienced adventure-seekers will be richly rewarded.

DIRECTIONS From Charlemont, go west on Rte. 2. Just before the road crosses a bridge over the Deerfield River, turn right onto a road marked with a "Rowe-Monroe" sign. In 2.3 miles, bear left at a fork and go 8 miles north on River Road. The trailhead is at a dirt parking area on the left, just south of the Monroe/Florida town line. The spacious Dunbar Brook Picnic Area, owned by a power company, is located down a short paved road across the street. It provides an alternate parking area from which a short singletrack spur trail leads 0.2 miles west up to the Dunbar Brook trailhead.

TRAIL Starting at the trailhead, follow the blue-blazed Dunbar Brook Trail as it briefly climbs a powerline access road. The trail then enters the woods to the right (west) and gently descends beneath hemlocks to the south bank of Dunbar Brook, where it rises and falls along the riverbank (do not take the stairs leading

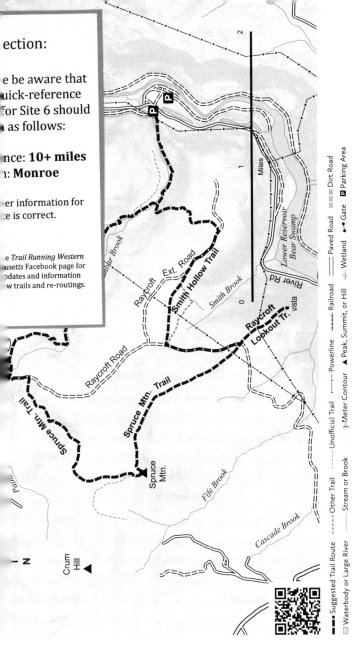

ection:

e be aware that
uick-reference
for Site 6 should
as follows:

nce: **10+ miles**
n: **Monroe**

er information for
e is correct.

e *Trail Running Western
ousetts* Facebook page for
odates and information
w trails and re-routings.

Smith Hollow Trail

Raycroft Ext. Road

Smith Brook

Raycroft Road

Raycroft
Lookout Tr.

vista

Spruce Mtn. Trail

Spruce Mtn. Trail

Spruce
Mtn.

Fife Brook

Cascade Brook

River Rd

Lower Reservoir
Bear Swamp

Miles

Crum
Hill

N

— ━ Suggested Trail Route
━━ Waterbody or Large River
------ Other Trail
─── Stream or Brook
------ Unofficial Trail
3-Meter Contour
•─•─ Powerline
•─•─•─ Railroad
━━━ Paved Road
=== Dirt Road
⬩ Wetland
•─⟍ Gate
▲ Peak, Summit, or Hill
P Parking Area

down to a dam on the right). In just under 1 mile, take a left on Smith Hollow Trail and begin the loop portion with a very steep ascent of the hillside to the south (where some of the trees are *very* old). In 0.3 miles, the grade lessens and you pass to the left of a lean-to called Ridge Shelter.

From the shelter, the now-wider trail continues climbing to a junction with a dirt road called Raycroft Extension Road. Turn right and follow this service road for about 0.25 miles. Stay straight at a junction, where the Smith Hollow Trail (a possible alternate route) descends left to Smith Hollow Shelter. Continue at a gentle grade to Raycroft Road (dirt). Go left on the road, pass the upper end of the Smith Hollow Trail on the left, and ascend gradually for about 0.6 miles to a height of land just after passing beneath a powerline.

Turn left here for a very worthwhile out-and-back trip. The trail heads southeast up and over Hunt Hill and past an open powerline swath for 0.5 miles to Raycroft Lookout, a vista 1,100 feet above the Deerfield River gorge. Return back the way you came.

From the 4-way intersection on Raycroft Road, take Spruce Mountain Trail northwest up the slope. In 0.1 miles, the trail crosses beneath a powerline, then continues climbing over rocky and rooty ground along a wide but somewhat overgrown path for 1 mile to a forested sub-summit just east of Spruce Mountain. In another 0.4 miles, you arrive at the 2,730-ft. summit of Spruce Mountain, where a short spur path leads west to a ledge with a south-facing view.

Now begin the long descent by following Spruce Mountain Trail to the north. The footing can be tricky in places for a while, with plentiful roots and mossy rocks, but it gets better further down. In 0.5 miles, cross over a wide snowmobile route, staying on the narrow, blue-blazed trail. At 1.25 miles from the top, you reach an intersection with Raycroft Road. Go left and descend for 0.1 miles to a junction with Dunbar Brook Trail, which leads to the right just after the road crosses a bridge. The descent along this trail can be extremely fun, especially the portions beneath pine and hemlock where the soft needle litter feels nice underfoot after the rockier parts higher up. At one point, the trail passes right below a huge glacial erratic boulder before dropping steeply down to the edge of Dunbar Brook. Lower down, cross Parsonage Brook on a wooden bridge, pass under a powerline, and reach Dunbar Brook Shelter. Stay left on the trail before the shelter and cross Haley Brook on a narrow bridge.

At 2.3 miles from Raycroft Road, the trail reaches a crossing of Dunbar Brook that requires wading through the water. Take extra care if the flow is strong. (As of this writing, there are plans to rebuild a bridge at this crossing.) The trail climbs the riverbank on the other side and immediately reaches the junction with Smith Hollow Trail, closing the loop portion of your run. Go left here and return to the parking area.

NEARBY Pelham Lake Park in Rowe, the Hoosac Range Trail in North Adams, and Mohawk Trail State Forest in Charlemont—each featured in this guide—are all nearby.

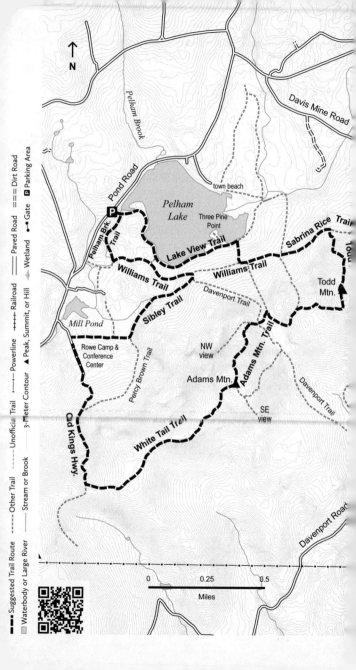

Pelham Lake Park

DISTANCE 5.5 Miles **TOWN** Rowe
DIFFICULTY RATING Moderate/Challenging
TRAIL STYLE Lollipop Loop **TRAIL TYPE** Singletrack

Pelham Lake Park in Rowe is a town-owned property featuring a lightly used network of first-rate singletrack hiking trails and snowmobile paths. The route described here loops up over several peaks of a low mountain ridge and skirts the edge of a lake. The footing varies widely throughout, ranging from soft and gentle in some areas to rocky and rooty in others. Appealing elements of this trail run include the peaceful setting, several worthwhile vistas, and a possible post-run dip in or picnic by the lake in a quaint, quiet, and remote Berkshire town.

DIRECTIONS From Rte. 2 west of Charlemont, go 2.5 miles northwest on Zoar Road. At a 3-way junction, turn right on Rowe Road and go 3.8 miles to the village of Rowe. Turn right on Pond Road and go 0.35 miles to a small, rooty parking area on the right, just before Pelham Lake.

TRAIL Starting at the parking area, take the Lake View Trail over a bridge across Pelham Brook. On the other side of the bridge, stay left at a junction and follow Lake View Trail for about 0.7 miles around the southern shore of Pelham Lake. After passing a short spur out to Three Pine Point, take a right on Adams Mountain Trail and begin climbing at a moderate grade. In about 0.1 miles, go left on Williams Trail, ascending at a gentle grade. In about 0.2 miles, go straight at a 4-way junction on Sabrina Rice Trail and continue east, climbing gradually, for about 0.25 miles. Turn right on Todd Mountain Trail and climb steeply for 0.3 miles to the wooded summit. Though rough and rooty in this section, the trail is well maintained, well marked, and easy to follow.

From the top of Todd Mountain, descend south and then west on Todd Mountain Trail for 0.3 miles. Undulating across the ridge, pass the upper ends of the Saddle Brook and Adams Mountain Trails, then arrive at a 4-way intersection. Continue straight and climb a short distance to a 3-way junction.

Optional Extension Take a right and follow Northwest View Trail about 0.2 miles across the north slope of the mountain out to a northward vista, then return the same way.

From the Northwest View Trail junction, climb steeply on Adams Mountain Trail for 0.3 miles to the wooded summit of Adams Mountain.

Optional Extension Take the Southeast View Trail steeply down to a ledge where there is an excellent view out over the Deerfield River valley to the south, then return to the summit.

From the top, descend southwest on White Tail Trail. The grade is moderate at first, but it soon levels off as the trail follows the more or less level crest of the ridge. At 0.8 miles from the summit, take a right and descend steeply along the sometimes rough Old Kings Highway for 0.5 miles to the Rowe Conference Center. Then follow the access road downhill for 0.25 miles. Turn right on Sibley Trail and go east over mostly gentle terrain for 0.7 miles, passing junctions with South Trail and Percy Brown Trail along the way. Just past the wooden lean-to shelter, go left on Williams Trail and descend gently over mostly smooth, packed dirt for 0.4 miles. Turn right on Pelham Brook Trail and ascend gently along the brook for about 0.2 miles to the bridge by the parking area.

NEARBY Several miles south in Charlemont, the Charlemont Trails network links miles of non-motorized recreational trails in the town with access points at the Warfield House at Valley View Farm, Berkshire East, and Zoar Outdoor.

DISTANCE 4.75 Miles   **TOWN** Charlemont/Savoy
DIFFICULTY RATING Moderate/Challenging
TRAIL STYLE Loop   **TRAIL TYPE** Singletrack

The northern part of Mohawk Trail State Forest sits on a sharp peninsula at the confluence of the Deerfield River and the Cold River. There are two good options for trail run loops at this site: The shorter one is quite easy, while the longer one requires an arduous, sustained hill climb. Portions of the routes described here pass through towering stands of old-growth forest, with some of the tallest white pine trees in the region.

DIRECTIONS From Charlemont, go about 4 miles west on Rte. 2 to the well-signed entrance road on the right. There is a large dirt parking area right along Rte. 2. Alternatively, there is parking on the other side of the bridge, just past the fee station.

TRAIL Starting at the parking area, cross the bridge over the Cold River. Bear right and follow the paved road past a gate, after which the road turns to dirt. At a signed junction, the singletrack Mahican-Mohawk (M/M) Trail veers left off the road. This portion of the trail has very nice, soft footing and is easy to run along. Well-marked with both white blazes and occasional yellow circles, it climbs gently over a low upland ridge. In about 0.5 miles, the trail intersects a dirt road on a high floodplain terrace above the Deerfield River.

Take a left and go north along the dirt road. Soon you arrive at a 3-way road junction. Follow the M/M Trail, first left up a different dirt road and then right off that road back onto a singletrack trail. In about 0.25 miles, you arrive at a 3-way junction

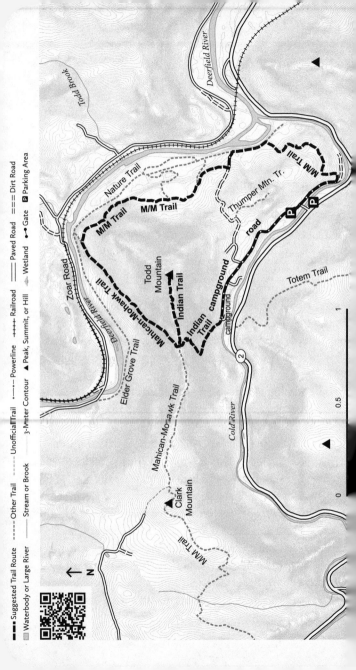

Suggested Trail Route ---- Other Trail ----- Unofficial Trail +++ Powerline --- Paved Road === Dirt Road
—— Waterbody or Large River —— Stream or Brook ——— 3-Meter Contour ▲ Peak, Summit, or Hill ⊸ Gate P Parking Area

N

Todd Brook

Deerfield River

Nature Trail

M/M Trail

M/M Trail

Zoar Road

Deerfield River

Mahican-Mohawk Trail

Elder Grove Trail

Todd Mountain

Indian Trail

Indian Trail

Thumper Mtn. Tr.

road

M/M Trail

campground

campground

P   P

Totem Trail

Cold River

Mahican-Mohawk Trail

Clark Mountain

M/M Trail

0   0.5   1

at the southern edge of a field. Go left (north) across the field on the M/M Trail. The gently undulating path across the field is usually mowed and makes for a particularly scenic stretch of this run, with the forested slope of Todd Mountain looming above.

Optional Trim For anyone seeking a shorter, easier run, an option is to take a right at the far end of the field and circle back around the peninsula on the Nature Trail, making a figure-8 loop. This pleasant route totals around 3.5 miles.

At the northern end of the field, follow the M/M Trail left back into the woods. It rises and falls as it traverses the bouldery northeastern slope of Todd Mountain. At a 3-way junction, a trail leads down to the right. Go left here and keep following the M/M Trail. The trail now ascends diagonally across the northern slope of Todd Mountain at a remarkably steady grade. This is a strenuous climb for even the most experienced runners. In less than a mile, it gains nearly 800 feet in elevation and finally arrives at a 4-way intersection in the saddle along the ridge between Todd Mountain and Clark Mountain.

Leaving the M/M Trail now, go left and follow Indian Trail about 0.5 miles up to the two peaks of Todd Mountain. Along the way, you pass over semi-open ledges with nice views to the south. At the eastern summit (1,697 ft.), there is a ledge with a limited view to the southeast. Turn back here and retrace your route back to the saddle.

Optional Extension If you would like to extend your run another 2 miles, go west along the M/M Trail about 0.8 miles up the narrow ridge to the 1,919-ft. summit of Clark Mountain. It is forested most of the way, but the trail is nice and passes through a variety of forest types.

Back at the saddle, head south on the Indian Trail. This trail drops very steeply down the south side of the ridge, descending about 700 feet in only 0.3 miles. The footing is poor and care should be taken both to not fall and to not cause further erosion. At the bottom, the trail comes out along the paved campground road. Go left here and follow the road about 0.7 miles back to the bridge at the forest entrance.

NEARBY About 5 miles south, a network of woods roads and trails—including more than six miles of singletrack—runs through Kenneth Dubuque Forest in Hawley.

DISTANCE 4.5 Miles **TOWN** Windsor

DIFFICULTY RATING Moderate **TRAIL STYLE** Figure-8 Loop

TRAIL TYPE Singletrack/Doubletrack

Notchview Reservation, owned and managed by The Trustees of Reservations (TTOR), is one of the premier cross-country skiing destinations in the Berkshires. Despite the property's primary focus on winter use, the trails are open during other seasons, and the occasional trail race has been held here. The described route follows parts of the route of one such 10K race. Trails at Notchview are mostly wide and uncrowded, but they are often wet in places and many are not maintained for summer recreation. In general, mid-summer is a challenging time for running since the vegetation can be waist-high in places, often obscuring the trails and any wet areas. The best season for running at Notchview is probably mid-to-late fall, before the snow flies but after early frosts have caused much of the vegetation to die back a bit.

DIRECTIONS From Northampton, go about 30 miles west on Rte. 9. Near the top of a long rise in Windsor, look for the small green TTOR sign on the right for the Notchview Reservation. Turn in and go right (south) a few hundred feet to the very large parking area by the Arthur A. Budd Visitor Center. From Pittsfield, Notchview is about 12 miles east on Rte. 9.

TRAIL From the trailhead kiosk in front of the visitor center building, go southeast across the open field on the mowed Circuit Trail. The path joins a dirt road near a house, follows the edge of the woods a short distance, then enters the woods and passes several cross-country ski trails coming down the hill on the left. About 0.4 miles from the start, veer right on the Mixed Woods Trail at junction #4 and descend at a gentle grade over undulating terrain for 0.3 miles. At a junction with a dirt road, go left. At the next junction, veer left and follow the road up the hill with an open field on the right. At a 4-way intersection, continue straight on the Minor Trail (a wide woods road). Staying straight at several junctions that come in quick succession, go north about 0.5 miles to a junction (#11) with Shaw Road, a wide dirt road.

The next section is a highlight of this run and of a visit to Notchview in general. Take a right on Shaw Road to begin a 2-mile lollipop loop. Descend east on Shaw Road for 0.3 miles to a junction (#12), then continue east another 0.25 miles over rolling terrain to an unmarked junction at the edge of the property. Turn left and pass through an old stone gate. The Bumpus Trail rises gradually between two rows of old maple trees through an open pasture for 0.5 miles to a junction (#15) at the upper edge of the field. There are excellent views to the east from this section of trail. Turn left on Bates Road and descend relatively steeply for 0.3 miles back to junction #12. Turn left and climb Shaw Road to junction #11.

Ascend at a gentle grade along Shaw Road for 0.5 miles. At junction #10, turn left on Circuit Trail. At junction #2, turn right on Circuit Trail and go about 0.3 miles to junction #1. Turn left and follow Circuit Trail for about 0.25 miles down to the visitor center, passing the lower ends of several trails on the hillside to the left.

Optional Extensions When the vegetation has died back some in the fall, the trails to remoter portions of the property can be fun to run. Some possible trails to use for extensions include Windsor Trail, Judges Hill Trail, and the short but mossy and pleasant Bridge

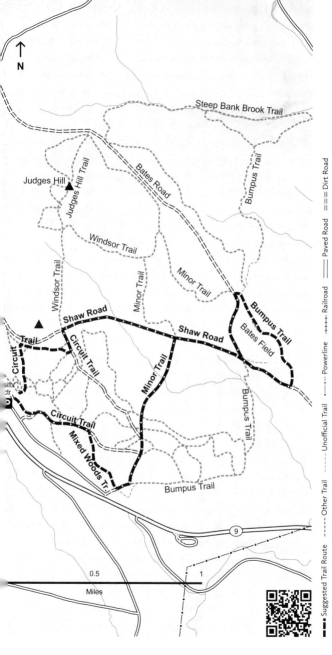

N

Steep Bank Brook Trail

Judges Hill ▲

Judges Hill Trail

Bates Road

Bumpus Trail

Windsor Trail

Windsor Trail

Minor Trail

Minor Trail

▲

Shaw Road

Circuit Trail

Shaw Road

Bumpus Trail

Bates Field

Circuit Trail

sitor
tr

Minor Trail

Circuit Trail

Bumpus Trail

Mixed Woods Tr.

Bumpus Trail

9

0.5

1

Miles

--- Suggested Trail Route   ----- Other Trail   ----- Unofficial Trail   —— Paved Road   === Dirt Road

—— Waterbody or Large River   —— Stream or Brook   ++++ Railroad   •—• Powerline   ⚓ Wetland   •— Gate   🅿 Parking Area

▲ Peak, Summit, or Hill   —— 3-Meter Contour

Trail. The northern extension of the Bumpus Trail can be difficult to find at the top of Bates Field, but—combined with the upper part of the Steep Bank Brook Trail—it makes a good longer route for experienced runners who are comfortable with rougher trails and backcountry route-finding.

NEARBY A few miles to the northeast, several miles of trails start at River Road in Windsor State Forest, including one to the scenic ravine and cascades of Windsor Jambs Brook.

DISTANCE 4–5 Miles **TOWN** Pittsfield/Dalton
DIFFICULTY RATING Moderate **TRAIL STYLE** Lollipop Loop
TRAIL TYPE Singletrack/Doubletrack/Dirt Road

Wedged into a forested triangle of land framed by Rte. 9, Rte. 8, and Gulf Road, a conservation property called The Boulders offers some very fine trail running immediately adjacent to downtown Dalton. The described loop is mostly easy-to-moderate doubletrack, following old woods roads and occasional singletrack around the property. The trail network is dense, with many connecting trails and spurs. All are good for running. Some trails are marked by colored wooden blocks on trees, and named accordingly. It can be easy to get turned around, but it's difficult to ever *really* get lost at The Boulders since roads bound it on all sides.

DIRECTIONS From Main Street (Rte. 9/Rte. 8) in Dalton, take Carson Avenue 0.3 miles north to High Street. Turn left and go about 0.7 miles west on High Street (which turns into Gulf Road) to a small parking area for the Appalachian Trail on the right side of Gulf Road, just past the Dalton town garage. There is space here for 4–5 vehicles.

TRAIL Starting at the parking area, cross Gulf Road and find the trailhead, which features a sign and map for The Boulders. Take the narrow trail a short distance south into the woods. At a junction, go right and follow the trail west through the woods along the top of a slope. Soon you come to an intersection with a wider trail (right leads back out to the road, left down a steep, eroded gully). Go straight and descend diagonally along the slope on

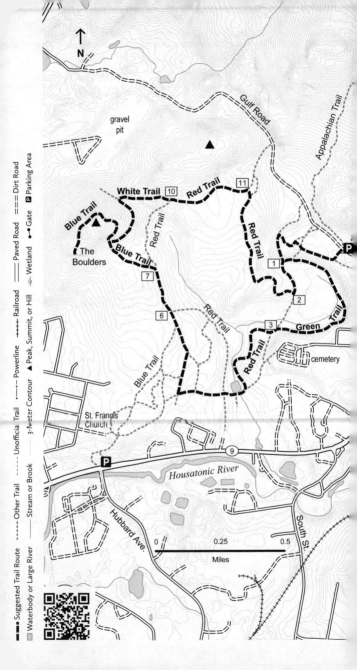

Along the Red Trail at The Boulders.

a singletrack trail. At a junction with a mostly level woods road at the bottom, go left. In about 0.2 miles, you come to a 3-way junction marked #1. This is the start of the loop portion.

Taking a right on the Green Trail, immediately cross a wooden bridge and quickly come to a 3-way junction (#2). Go right on the Red Trail and climb at a gentle grade for about 0.5 miles along the wide trail to another 3-way junction (#11). The right fork leads out to Gulf Road on the Gray Trail. Staying on the Red Trail, go left across a level area to another 3-way junction (#10). Take a right here on the White Trail. You quickly come to an unmarked 3-way junction. Take a sharp left to stay on the White Trail, and follow a gradual curve up to the right to another unmarked 3-way junction. Go right on the Blue Trail for an out-and-back spur. Climbing at steady grade, the trail curves left around the top of a 1,375-foot high hill and arrives at a dead-end bulb. From here, a short spur path leads over to Wizard's Glen, where scattered large boulders and ledges offer partial views south and west across the valley.

Return to the junction and go straight on the Blue Trail,

gradually descending south. Stay straight at the next two junctions (#7 and #6, respectively), both with the Red Trail. Then, leaving the Blue Trail, bear left, right, and left at the next three unmarked junctions. At the fourth unmarked junction, turn sharply left. Now heading east, go straight at a 4-way intersection and descend slightly to the southern edge of a small pond. After passing the pond, turn left at an unmarked junction and head north. Veer right past a pair of utility sheds marked with "High Voltage" signs and enter a section of dark conifer woods. Go straight at a 4-way intersection (#3) and follow the Green Trail as it gradually curves around to the left. In 0.7 miles you arrive back at junction #1, closing the loop portion of the run. From there, take a right to return back the way you came in.

> *Alternate Options* The footing along the Red Trail is excellent the entire way, and a shorter lollipop loop using just that trail would make a great 3–4 mile run, from any of the entrances to the Boulders. There are also several meandering singletrack mountain bike trails worth exploring in the southern portion of the property.

NEARBY From the Gulf Road trailhead, run north on the Appalachian Trail (AT) for about 3.5 miles up to remote Gore Pond. If you go an additional 2 miles north on the AT, you will come to the top of Cheshire Cobble, where there is a spectacular view of Mt. Greylock. Alternatively, run a challenging 6.3-mile AT out-and-back to Warner Hill from Grange Hall Road in Dalton, about 3 miles to the southeast.

DISTANCE 9 Miles   **TOWN** Pittsfield/Lanesborough/Hancock
DIFFICULTY RATING Challenging
TRAIL STYLE Loop   **TRAIL TYPE** Singletrack

The central portion of Pittsfield State Forest contains a staggering number of marked and unmarked trails, and it certainly invites multiple visits to explore more. There are ponds and swamps and excellent vistas from the heights of the Taconic Ridge. The route described here includes several miles of gently winding mountain bike trails in the lower portion, which serve as a nice warm-up for the challenging climb to the ridge that comes later.

There are many possible variations on this run. One particularly notable option is to use the newer version of the Turner Trail for ascending or descending the ridge. Built by mountain bikers, this sinuous trail utilizes many switchbacks to climb to the ridge at a continuously gentle grade. The forest is also heavily used by off-road vehicles (ORVs), and you will likely hear them. If you generally stay on the singletrack trails and narrower doubletrack trails, however, you shouldn't need to dodge any.

DIRECTIONS From Rte. 7 in Pittsfield, take West Street about 2.6 miles west. Take a right on Churchill Street and go north for 1.75 miles. Turn left on Cascade Street and go 0.5 miles west. Turn right and enter Pittsfield State Forest. This loop can be started either from the small paved parking lot just to the left of the entrance (as described) or from the large, unpaved Lulu Brook picnic area parking lot about 0.5 miles straight ahead up the park road.

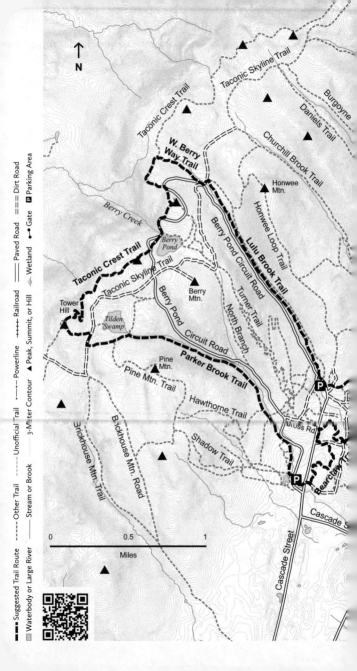

TRAIL Take the unnamed singletrack trail that enters the woods just east of the parking area. Soon you cross the paved Berry Pond Circuit Road. From here, stay on singletrack trail all the way back to a junction with the same road further north. There are many confusing intersections, but if you just keep taking lefts on singletrack except for two noted short doubletrack sections, you should get there without getting lost.

Just after entering the woods, take a left (north) on Bearclaw Trail. The trail meanders back and forth over gentle, undulating terrain. At an old road, go straight (north) across and follow the trail marked "To Deer Hill Trail" to a junction near the eastern end of Cross Road. Here, continue on Deer Hill Trail, which swings southeast and arrives at a 5-way intersection. Take a left and follow Deer Hill Trail north. For a few hundred feet it is coincident with a doubletrack road, then it bears right and crosses Lulu Brook on boardwalk bridges. It soon stays left at a junction, then gently climbs north to a dirt road. It goes left on the road very briefly, then turns right. It ambles back and forth for a while, crossing several junctions with wider trails along the way, and ends at the paved Berry Pond Circuit Road just east of the Lulu Brook parking area.

Optional Extension The route described stays as close as possible to the paved road on singletrack trail, but you can extend the run about a mile by adding on a complex loop on the Bearclaw and Whirlpool Trails. This scenic route passes near a beaver pond along Lulu Brook and a location called the Whirlpool, where a small brook disappears underground. Allow some extra time for route-finding if you choose this option; several unmarked trails branch off from it and head south or east.

Now climb to the ridge via Lulu Brook Trail along the right (east) bank of Lulu Brook. Starting at a gate on the east side of the road northeast of the Lulu Brook parking area, the trail be-

Running along (a short road section of) the Taconic Crest Trail at Pittsfield State Forest.

gins climbing at a moderate grade. (The left leg of the wider and straighter Honwee Loop Trail is always just uphill to the right, and sometimes even in view; this trail would make a possible alternative if the Lulu Brook Trail is too wet, icy, or leafy). The trail very quickly arrives at Lulu Cascade, an attractive small waterfall, then ascends steeply to the right of it.

About 1.5 miles from the trailhead, go left at an unmarked junction (the Honwee Loop Trail is to the right). You quickly come to a rough ORV trail. Cross the brook on the ORV trail and ascend to a junction with Berry Pond Circuit Road. Go uphill along the paved road for about 100 feet, then veer right back into the woods on an unmarked upper extension of the Lulu Brook Trail called William Berry Way Trail. Ascend at a gentle grade for about 0.3 miles to an unmarked junction. Go left and follow the Taconic Crest Trail (blazed with distinctive blue diamond markers) and climb for about 0.5 miles to a junction with the paved road. Go right and almost immediately veer right off the road and climb along the right side of an open area called Azalea Field. Near the top of Berry Hill, follow the Taconic Crest Trail right at an unmarked junction (going left leads to a nice view to the north). Descend briefly and reach the road, where there is a stunning, sweeping view southeast into New York.

Follow the road down to Berry Pond. Stay right at the pond, and then immediately veer left onto a dirt road. Climbing slowly, pass several campsites and then re-cross the paved road. The Taconic Crest Trail enters the woods on the south side of the road at a sign that says "Foot Path" and heads south. It rises and falls over a hill and then climbs Tower Hill via switchbacks.

At the top of Tower Hill, leave the Taconic Crest Trail by taking a left. Descend to the Taconic Skyline Trail (wide and used by ORVs) for 0.25 miles on a narrow path that can be overgrown in summer; gaiters would be a good idea here. Turn right and go 400 feet on the Taconic Skyline Trail. Turn left at an easily overlooked junction and descend east at a gentle grade. In 0.2 miles, pass a junction with Pine Mountain Trail leading uphill to the right. In another 0.2 miles you arrive at the shore of Tilden Swamp (now a beaver pond).

Go east down Parker Brook Trail for about 1.5 miles. There are a few steep and rough sections, but in general the grade is moderate and the footing good. Near the bottom, pass several junctions with trails leading off to the right and a bridge leading left to campsites across the brook. Continuing straight, the trail becomes a part of the Tranquility Trail, a network of paved pathways. Stay straight at all junctions. At the bottom, take a left out to the parking area.

NEARBY There are many other great running trails at Pittsfield State Forest, on all sides of the route described here.

DISTANCE 6.5 Miles   **TOWN** Hancock

DIFFICULTY RATING Challenging   **TRAIL STYLE** Lollipop Loop

TRAIL TYPE Singletrack/Doubletrack

Shaker Mountain, also known as Mt. Sinai, lies on the eastern side of the Taconic Range in the southern portion of Pittsfield State Forest. A moderately challenging trail run crosses over both this peak and an adjacent hill called Holy Mount on a mix of singletrack, doubletrack, and old woods roads. Portions of the lollipop loop described here follow a route called the Shaker Trail/Scout Trail and are blazed with metal markers featuring white circles inside a green triangle, but the markings are inconsistent and should not be relied on. This run passes several marked historic sites and features of interest, and is runnable for all but the steepest portions of the ascent of Shaker Mountain. Several longer options are also possible, utilizing the network of hiking trails and both motorized and non-motorized multi-use trails.

DIRECTIONS From Rte. 7 in Pittsfield, go 4.6 miles west on Rte. 20 to a paved parking pullover on the right, where the road makes a curve to the left across the street from Hancock Shaker Village.

TRAIL From the parking area, find the trailhead at the metal gate. Head north into the woods on the wide North Family Trail, aka West Road (may not be marked), climbing at a gentle grade. In about 0.2 miles, just after passing to the left of Shaker Reservoir pond, you pass a junction with a grassy road on the right that leads southeast across farm fields to Hancock

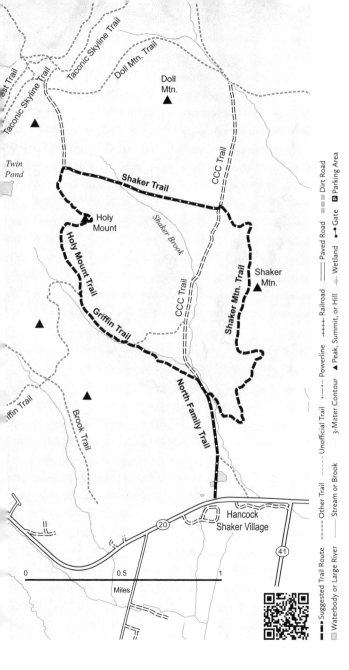

Doll Mtn.

Taconic Skyline Trail
Taconic Skyline Trail
Taconic Skyline Trail
Doll Mtn. Trail
est Trail

Twin Pond

Shaker Trail

Holy Mount

Holy Mount Trail

Griffin Trail

CCC Trail

Shaker Brook

CCC Trail

Shaker Mtn. Trail

Shaker Mtn.

North Family Trail

iffin Trail

Brook Trail

Hancock Shaker Village

20

41

0   0.5   1

Miles

Suggested Trail Route · · · · · Other Trail · · · · · · Unofficial Trail +--+-- Powerline ——— Railroad === Dirt Road ——— Paved Road ——— Wetland •—• Gate 🅿 Parking Area

Waterbody or Large River ——— Stream or Brook   3-Meter Contour ▲ Peak, Summit, or Hill

Shaker Village (admission fee required). At about 0.4 miles from the gate, you reach a junction just upstream from a dam along Shaker Brook.

Go right on the Shaker Trail and cross the brook on a wooden bridge. On the other side of the brook, bear right and head southeast along the brook. After passing by several marked historical sites on the right, bear left on the Shaker Mtn. Trail at a Y-junction, pass through a wooden gate, and begin climbing at an easy grade. In a short distance, turn sharply left and start the climb of Shaker Mountain. The climb is fairly steep, but the trail switches back and forth several times on the way up. At a fork in the trail, bear left. Soon after the fork, the trail crosses a very steep road along a utility line. It then swings left and re-crosses the utility line road higher up. After another sustained climb, the trail levels off and crosses a shrubby area near the top of the forested mountain. Look for an interpretive sign here about a historic Shaker site. From the top, descend the northwest side at a moderate grade about 0.5 miles to a complex junction of several trails and heavily eroded roads.

At the junction, go left for about 100 yards on the CCC Trail, then take an immediate right on Shaker Trail. This wide old road is open to motorized traffic and is eroded and wet in places. Follow the road west for about 0.75 miles, relatively level at first and then gradually rising. An intermittent stream along this section may require a water crossing after heavy rains. You arrive at a T-intersection where the road bears right. Go left on the narrower Holy Mount Trail and begin climbing at a moderate grade up the northwest slope of Holy Mount. During summer, the trail can be somewhat overgrown with raspberry brambles in this section, and gaiters may be called for. In about 0.3 miles, near the top, a short side trail leads left to an impressively intact stone wall. The trail swings right and descends steeply but with good footing down the south slope of the hill. In about 0.5 miles it reaches a natural amphitheater on the left called the Sacred Gap. After crossing the outlet stream of the amphitheater's spring, the trail levels out slightly and reaches a junction with the Griffin Trail in about 0.5 miles.

Go left and follow Griffin Trail, a rough old road of loose rocks and soft dirt, southeast along a stream. In 0.3 miles you come to a 3-way intersection where the CCC Trail leads left. Bear right and follow North Family Trail down to the southeast, crossing a small stream along the way. In about 0.3 miles you arrive back at the junction with Shaker Trail, completing the loop portion of the run. Follow North Family Trail back out the way you came to return to the parking area along Rte. 20.

NEARBY Just to the west of this site, the scenic and well-marked Taconic Crest Trail runs north for 35 miles from Rte. 20 in Hancock to Petersburgh, New York.

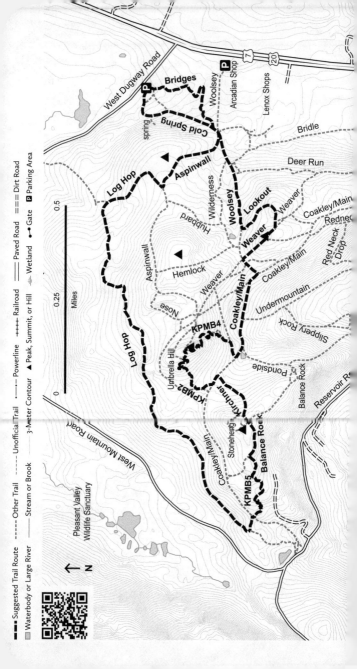

DISTANCE 4 Miles TOWN Lenox

DIFFICULTY RATING Moderate TRAIL STYLE Loop

TRAIL TYPE Singletrack/Doubletrack

Only a few minutes south of the city of Pittsfield, John Drummond Kennedy Park in Lenox is an easily accessible property with many miles of non-motorized recreational trails. Situated along a series of hills east of Yokun Ridge and west of Rte. 7, it is terrific for trail running, with many possible loop options. The route described here provides a sampling of some of the different types of terrain and features in the northern portion of the park.

DIRECTIONS From exit 2 off I-90, take Rte. 20 north for 8 miles. Turn left on West Dugway Road and go 0.15 miles west. Turn left into the dirt parking area. Alternate parking is possible nearby at the Arcadian Shop along Rte. 7 and near the Church on the Hill off of Rte. 7A.

TRAIL From the parking area, take the Bridges Trail due south and immediately bear left at a junction. This singletrack route climbs gently for about 0.3 miles through a forest festooned with hardy kiwifruit vines. At a junction with Cold Spring Trail, go left for about 50 feet to a 5-way junction. Go right on Woolsey Trail, then immediately take another right on Aspinwall Trail. Climb north at a gentle grade on Aspinwall for 0.25 miles.

Turn right on Log Hop Trail and descend gradually for 0.2 miles. Stay left at a junction, then follow Log Hop west, undulating along the hillside for 1.1 miles and hopping over several of the namesake logs along the way. At a junction, go left for 200 feet to a junction with the wide Coakley/Main Trail. Go right and take an immediate left onto KPMB5. This narrow trail squiggles gently up the slope via a series of tight switchbacks for 0.25 miles. Go right on Balance Rock across a level ridge for 0.1 miles. Stay left at a fork, then straight at a 4-way intersection.

> *Optional Extensions* At the intersection an easy, short loop on the left called Stonehenge Trail circles around old concrete foundations. An easy out-and-back from the same intersection leads right to the Balance Rock boulder.

Descend at a moderate grade on Kirchner Trail to Coakley/Main. Go left and briefly climb to a junction. Go right for about 150 feet to a junction with Weaver Olympics Trail, then take another right, go right for 100 feet, and then take another right. Climb Umbrella Hill via switchbacks on the narrow KPMB2 Trail, then take a right at the top and go about 100 feet east to a junction with the top of KPMB4. Descend at a moderate grade on this technical and very fun trail, which makes broad swoops across a steep hillside. It forks briefly near the bottom; either choice works. Near the bottom, bear right at a junction and return to Coakley/Main.

Turn left and descend past a small pond and junctions with the Pondside and Undermountain Trails on the right, then climb gradually for about 0.2 miles, bearing right where Aspinwall descends sharply from the left. Turn left on Woolsey, cross Cutoff Trail, and then take a right on Weaver Olympics. Climb steeply to the gazebo at the top of the hill, then descend on Lookout, which hooks left back around to Woolsey. Turn right and follow Woolsey for 0.25 miles to the 4-way intersection that started your loop. Take a left on Cold Spring and descend 0.25 miles north back to the parking lot, passing the stone-lined spring along the way.

NEARBY Southern parts of the park also feature nice trails. Several recommended ones include Deer Run, Red Neck, and Red Neck Drop, as well as those to the picnic area at the former site of the Aspinwall Hotel just north of the Church on the Hill parking area.

14 Yokun Ridge

DISTANCE 6+ Miles   **TOWNS:** Stockbridge/Lenox/Richmond
DIFFICULTY RATING Moderate   **TRAIL STYLE** Lollipop/Figure-8 Loop
TRAIL TYPE Singletrack/Doubletrack

Yokun Ridge traces an arc through the center of the Housatonic River valley, separating the towns of Lenox and Stockbridge from Richmond and West Stockbridge. The northern half is also known as Lenox Mountain and the southern part is called West Stockbridge Mountain. The Berkshire Natural Resources Council (BNRC) maintains a well-built network of trails near the middle of the ridge, and several loop run options are possible. The route described here includes sections on both sides of Richmond Mountain Road/Lenox Road and offers visitors a scenic, moderately challenging trail run over several peaks, past a small pond, and through a variety of forest types.

DIRECTIONS From Rte. 7A in the center of Lenox, take Rte. 183 west for 1.6 miles. Turn right on Richmond Mountain Road and go west for 0.8 miles to a small parking area on the right. There is space here for 4–5 vehicles. There is also parking available another 0.5 miles up the road at Olivia's Overlook.

TRAIL From the gate at the parking area, follow Old Baldhead Road uphill at a moderate grade for 0.3 miles to Monks Pond. Turn left at the junction and go west a few hundred feet across the old dam to a junction, then turn left on the red-blazed Burbank Trail. This lovely trail leads southwest across the slope of Yokun Ridge, gently rising and falling for 0.7 miles as it makes its way to a 4-way intersection.

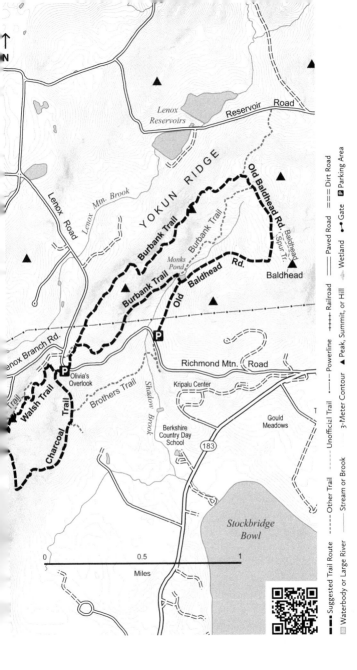

N

Lenox Reservoirs

Reservoir Road

YOKUN RIDGE

Lenox Mtn. Brook

Lenox Road

Burbank Trail

Old Baldhead Rd.

Baldhead Spur Tr.

Burbank Trail

Monks Pond

Burbank Trail

Old Baldhead Rd.

Baldhead

Lenox Branch Rd.

P

Olivia's Overlook

Richmond Mtn. Road

Kripalu Center

Gould Meadows

Walsh Trail

Brothers Trail

Shadow Brook

Charcoal Trail

Berkshire Country Day School

183

Stockbridge Bowl

0   0.5   1

Miles

- - - Suggested Trail Route
----- Other Trail
····· Unofficial Trail
—— Paved Road
=== Dirt Road
+++ Railroad
···· Powerline
—— Stream or Brook
≈ Wetland
•→ Gate
P Parking Area
▲ Peak, Summit, or Hill
— 3-Meter Contour
▓ Waterbody or Large River

Optional Trim To shorten the run, turn right on the Burbank Trail and complete the loop.

Turn left and follow the trail for 0.1 miles down to the paved road. Carefully cross the road to Olivia's Overlook, a parking area with an impressive view out over Stockbridge Bowl. Take the trail on the right side of the parking area through the clearing and across a wooden bridge to a junction and sign. Go left on Charcoal Trail and descend at a moderate grade for 0.25 miles to a junction with Brothers Trail (see alternate route below) and go right. In a few hundred feet, stay right at another junction and traverse the lower slope of the mountain. In about 0.5 miles the trail swings right and begins climbing more steeply to a junction at the crest of the ridge. Stay right at the junction and follow Walsh Trail past a vista and down the ridgeline to the north, passing several junctions with the parallel Ridge Trail on the left along the way. Back at the junction with the Charcoal Trail, go straight and return to Olivia's Overlook.

From Olivia's Overlook, carefully re-cross the road and return to the 4-way intersection. Go straight ahead on the red-blazed Burbank Trail and begin climbing northeast up Lenox Mountain at a gradual grade. At first, the trail stays to the west side of the ridge. Then, at about 0.5 miles, it swings right and climbs a short distance southeast to the crest of the ridge, which it then follows northeast. At about 1 mile from the junction there is a short spur path to a view on the left. From the vista, the trail descends gently for about 0.4 miles to a junction where a trail leads left toward Lenox Reservoirs. Go right and descend a narrow section of trail about 0.1 miles to another junction.

Optional Trim Turn right to stay on the Burbank Trail, which returns to the junction by Monks Pond in 0.7 miles. From there, go left and then right to return to the parking area.

Old Baldhead Road on the east side of Yokun Ridge.

From the junction, stay straight on the wide Old Baldhead Road, which has good footing and descends at a very gradual grade. In 0.25 miles you pass an unmarked junction with a narrow spur trail that leads 0.25 miles out to forested Baldface peak. Continue descending along Old Baldhead Road another 0.6 miles to Monks Pond. From there, follow the old road back down to the parking area.

Alternate Option To eliminate the "stick" portion of this lollipop loop, go south on the Brothers Trail from the parking area. This trail leads south from the road at the parking area; be careful crossing the road. In 0.1 miles it takes a hard right at a junction with a spur trail leading south. It then descends to Shadow Brook, which it crosses on stones, and climbs the opposite bank via a set of stone steps. Then it heads 0.5 miles across the slope to the junction with the Charcoal Pit Trail. From there, follow the rest of the loop as described above.

NEARBY Kennedy Park in Lenox, also featured in this book, offers many miles of moderately challenging trails, accessible from a number of entrances around the property's perimeter.

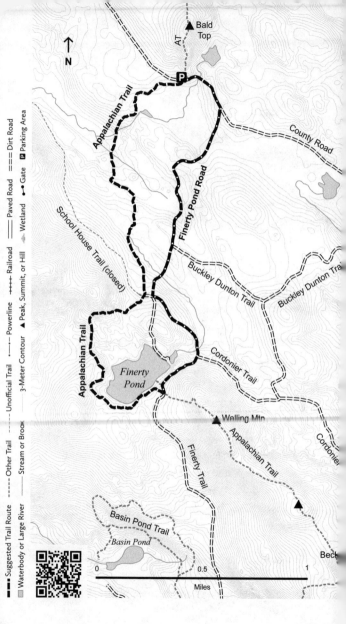

Appalachian Trail

Bald Top

AT

County Road

Finerty Pond Road

School House Trail (closed)

Buckley Dunton Trail

Buckley Dunton Tra

Cordonier Trail

Appalachian Trail

Finerty Pond

Welling Mtn

Appalachian Trail

Cordonier

Finerty Trail

Basin Pond Trail

Beck

Basin Pond

Suggested Trail Route ----- Other Trail ----- Unofficial Trail —— Paved Road === Dirt Road
Waterbody or Large River —— Stream or Brook ++++ Railroad ----- Powerline — Wetland • Gate P Parking Area
▲ Peak, Summit, or Hill —— 3-Meter Contour

↑ N

0   0.5   1
Miles

DISTANCE 4.5 Miles   **TOWN** Washington/Becket
DIFFICULTY RATING Moderate/Challenging
TRAIL STYLE Loop   **TRAIL TYPE** Singletrack/Doubletrack

October Mountain State Forest is a huge property that contains many trail running possibilities. The loop described here utilizes several different trail types. Remote and scenic Finerty Pond is the highlighted destination, but there are many other interesting features along the way, including forest, streams, beaver ponds, and marshes. Note: Some roads and trails shown on existing park maps, such as the Gorilla Trail, are closed.

DIRECTIONS The upper portion of October Mountain State Forest is currently only accessible from the east. From Rte. 8 in Becket, go west on County Road for 4 miles. The road turns to dirt as you enter the forest, and you pass a small off-road vehicle (ORV) parking pullout on the left. About 0.25 miles farther along, just after crossing the Appalachian Trail (AT), a small parking pullout on the right has space for about 3 vehicles (get there early!).

TRAIL Starting at the parking area, the white-blazed AT enters the woods south of the road and descends toward the northern shore of a marsh. Generally heading south, it crosses over several brooks and passes a few overlooks into marshes, but mostly it travels over rugged terrain through mixed forest. In about 0.9 miles, it begins a steady ascent of the slope to the south.

At about 1.2 miles, the AT reaches and crosses School House Trail (recently closed due to "unsafe conditions"). Keep following the AT as it crests a rise and begins to descend toward the northwestern shore of Finerty Pond. Before reaching the water, it swings around the western and southern shores. A dense mountain laurel thicket fringes much of the shoreline, but there is a small area where you can access the water directly. From the pond, take the AT about 300 feet uphill to a 4-way intersection where the AT continues straight, the multi-use Finerty Pond Road leads left, and the Finerty Trail leads right.

Optional Extension To add a strenuous but scenic extra 2.6 miles to your run, do an out-and-back spur southeast along the AT to the summit ridge of Walling and Becket Mountains. The ascent is gradual at first, then briefly quite steep as it climbs 0.5 miles to the 2,220-ft. summit of Walling Mountain. The views through the forest canopy are limited, but the trail along the narrow ridgeline itself is an attractive feature here, as it passes through a bright, boulder-strewn woodland with a soft, grassy understory and multiple fern glades. Continue rising and falling along the ridge to the summit of 2,200-ft. Becket Mountain, where there are concrete footings of a former fire tower. You can then turn back before the trail drops steeply down to Becket Road. Another option is to descend to Becket Road, turn right and follow it west for about 0.4 miles, and then take a right on Finerty Trail, which you can follow about 1.2 miles back up to Finerty Pond.

From the 4-way intersection, go north on Finerty Pond Road to a junction with Cordonier Trail and then go left. Cross a stream on a snowmobile bridge and then climb the slope to the west. You arrive at a 4-way intersection of the Finerty Pond Road and School House Trail about 100 feet east of where the AT crosses School House Trail.

Optional Extension Turning left here, a short climb and descent will bring you to the northern shore of Finerty Pond, where the road traverses the scenic shoreline for about 0.25 miles.

Turn right on the wide Finerty Pond Road and follow it for about a mile north to the ORV parking area along County Road, passing a junction with Buckley Dunton Trail on the right along the way. Then turn left and go about 0.2 miles on County Road to return back to the parking area.

NEARBY About 2 miles north, runners can make a fun lollipop loop using the Interpretive Trail and Outer Loop Trail at Washington Mountain Marsh Trail, though portions may be flooded at times, and the site may be difficult to reach before the dirt access road is graded in spring.

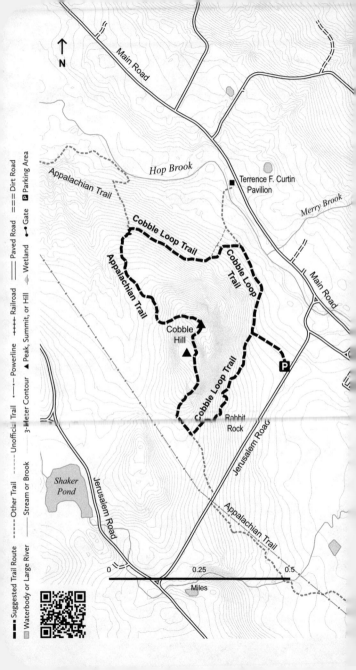

Legend:
- Suggested Trail Route
- Other Trail
- Unofficial Trail
- Powerline
- Railroad
- Paved Road
- Dirt Road
- Wetland
- Gate
- P Parking Area
- 3-Meter Contour
- Peak, Summit, or Hill
- Stream or Brook
- Waterbody or Large River

Main Road

Hop Brook

Appalachian Trail

Terrence F. Curtin Pavilion

Merry Brook

Cobble Loop Trail

Cobble Loop Trail

Appalachian Trail

Main Road

Cobble Hill

Cobble Loop Trail

P

Rabbit Rock

Jerusalem Road

Shaker Pond

Jerusalem Road

Appalachian Trail

0   0.25   0.5

Miles

DISTANCE 3 Miles **TOWN** Tyringham
DIFFICULTY RATING Moderate
TRAIL STYLE Loop **TRAIL TYPE** Singletrack

This short loop run includes a tremendous variety of scenery and features of ecological and geologic interest. The nutrient content of the rock is more calcium-rich than some of the surrounding area, and the plant communities reflect that difference. The property is owned and managed by The Trustees of Reservations (TTOR). The trail is very nicely constructed and maintained, and you can extend the mileage with several possible side trips on the Appalachian Trail (AT).

DIRECTIONS The large dirt parking area for this loop is located on Jerusalem Road about 0.5 miles south of the center of Tyringham.

TRAIL Leaving the parking area at a gate in the fence, the Cobble Loop Trail heads west across the open field for about 500 feet to a stone wall at the far end, where it arrives at a junction. Here the runner must make a decision. The loop can be taken in either direction, but this description describes the clockwise choice.

Southwest from the junction, the trail climbs gradually along the edge of the woods, with views east across the pastoral valley. In about 0.25 miles, it arrives at a vertical rock formation called Rabbit Rock. Made of weathered sandstone, it sticks up from the bedrock ledge and has been eroded into a shape that, from certain angles, very clearly resembles a sitting rabbit. Continuing south up the slope from Rabbit Rock, the trail climbs more steeply. It passes through a wooden gate and arrives at a marked junction with the AT just past a semi-open old field. Although the directions seem reversed at this location, left (south) is actually northbound on the AT while right (north) is southbound. Taking a right and coinciding with the AT for the next mile or so, the Cobble Loop Trail re-enters thicker woods and continues to climb the hill.

In a few hundred feet, the trail arrives at a ledge with a view to the east. Then it crosses over the first of Cobble Hill's two summits, where a short spur path on the right leads to an open ledge with a northeasterly view. Beyond the spur path and after a minor dip, the trail passes through a wooden gate, rises again slightly, and comes out into the open at a large ledge on the second summit, where there are broad views north and east across the Hop Brook valley.

Leaving the second summit, the trail drops to the northwest and passes through another wooden gate. The trail then bears left, descending gradually via switchbacks for about 0.5 miles to a junction where the Loop Trail leads right. Turning right here, the Cobble Loop Trail winds along the north side of the hill, passing the lower end of the shortcut trail in a few hundred feet. On its way back to the open fields, the Cobble Loop Trail passes several overgrown trails leading down to the left, all of which converge and lead about 0.3 miles to a town pavilion near the firehouse on Main Road in Tyringham.

As the Cobble Loop Trail traverses the lower slopes of the hill, it passes through an area of rich forest where spring ephemeral wildflowers grow in abundance, and the understory appears lush throughout the growing season (partly due to the presence of invasive shrubs, unfortunately). Seepy areas and small rill streams can sometimes cause the trail to be muddy along this section, especially in the spring and after recent rains. Then the trail passes through a wooden gate and emerges from the forest at a beautiful open meadow where trail maintainers mow a rolling path into the tall grass. After passing a junction with a mowed path leading sharply left, the trail eventually arrives back at the junction where you turn left to re-cross the field to the parking area.

Alternate Options Extra mileage can be added to this run by doing out-and-back extensions along the Appalachian Trail, heading either northbound or southbound. The northbound option departs from the Loop Trail at a sign about 0.25 miles uphill from Rabbit Rock. It descends the south side of Cobble Hill, crosses Jerusalem Road in about 0.25 miles, then continues heading downhill along the edges of an open field, eventually crossing Main Road in Tyringham about 1 mile from Jerusalem Road. The southbound option departs from the Loop Trail about 0.5 miles downhill to the north of the summit ledges. It continues downhill for a short distance and then veers westward (to the left) and traverses the base of the hill just above Hop Brook. About 0.5 miles from the junction, it turns left again and climbs southward up the slope toward Beartown State Forest. At about 1 mile from the junction, it crosses Jerusalem Road, then continues another two miles to the edge of a small open wetland. One other option for adding extra mileage is to run an out-and-back on the spur trail that leads down to the town pavilion from the Loop Trail.

NEARBY There are many miles of trails to run about 8 miles southwest at Beartown State Forest in the towns of Stockbridge, Great Barrington, and Monterey. Also, about 15 miles due south in New Marlborough and Sandisfield, a very scenic, moderately challenging 6–7-mile loop can be run on trails at Cookson State Forest and adjacent land trust properties just north of the Connecticut state line.

DISTANCE 3 Miles   **TOWNS:** Great Barrington/Stockbridge
DIFFICULTY RATING Moderate/Challenging
TRAIL STYLE Loop   **TRAIL TYPE** Singletrack

Monument Mountain is a prominent rocky ridge jutting above the Housatonic River valley. It is one of the most popular hiking destinations in the state, for a good reason. From its open summit ledges, it has fantastic views of the southern Berkshires, Mt. Greylock, the Taconic Range, and even the Catskills. The well-marked counterclockwise loop described here has some steep and rocky sections, but overall the footing is good and the trail is runnable for much of the way. There is a roughly 750-foot elevation change from the base to the summit of Squaw Peak, but it is mostly spread out over 1.5 miles on each side of the loop. The trail lies entirely on land owned and managed by The Trustees of Reservations (TTOR), who request a donation at the parking area. Due to the heavy visitation at the site, you may want to do this run on a weekday rather than a weekend.

DIRECTIONS From Rte. 102 in Stockbridge, take Rte. 7 south for 3 miles to the Monument Mountain parking area on the right. From Rte. 23 in Great Barrington, this lot is on the left 3 miles north on Rte. 7. If the main lot is full, a secondary parking area located about 0.25 miles north along Rte. 7 can be used.

TRAIL Starting at the map kiosk by the picnic area on the mountain's east side, take the yellow-blazed Hickey Trail north on fairly level terrain. In about 1,000 feet, pass a junction with a spur trail leading down to a secondary parking area. Keep going north. The trail begins to climb steadily, passing large boulders

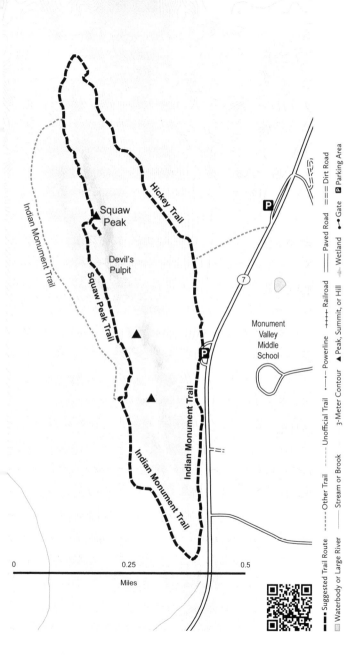

near the foot of a talus slope and crossing a small ravine on a log bridge. At 0.7 miles, the trail arrives at a 10-foot waterfall that may be dry in summer; a short spur path leads over to the cascade. The Hickey Trail climbs steeply to the right of the waterfall, then swings hard left and descends briefly. It crosses another log bridge over the stream above the waterfall, then climbs past boulders to a 3-way junction where Indian Mountain Trail leads to the right at Inscription Rock.

Go left (south) on Squaw Peak Trail and climb steeply over rugged, rocky terrain up the narrow summit ridge. The trail utilizes stone stairs in some places. Pass over the two peaks, at 1,642 ft. and 1,640 ft., respectively. Rocky outcrops jut above the pine trees and azalea shrubs, offering 360-degree views of the surrounding region. At 1.7 miles, you reach a junction with a spur path marked with a "Scenic Vista" sign. This trail leads left 0.1 miles out to a view over Devil's Pulpit, a column of loose quartzite rock separated from the main cliff. After the short side trip, continue south on the Squaw Peak Trail and descend the ridge at a moderate grade to a 3-way junction with Indian Mountain Trail.

Go left (south) on Indian Mountain Trail, a wide, old woods road. It descends steadily at first, then levels out before swinging hard left and curving around the south side of the ridge. From there, the trail narrows to singletrack and heads north at a gentle grade through the strip of woods between the steep ridge on the left and Rte. 7 on the right. The footing is somewhat rockier here. In 0.4 miles you arrive back at the parking lot.

NEARBY About 3 miles to the north along Rte. 7, from a trailhead by Goodrich Memorial footbridge at the end of Park Street in Stockbridge, you can run short, moderately difficult out-and-back spurs to Ice Glen and Laura's Tower, and a short lollipop loop around the flat Mary Flynn Trail along the river.

18 Jug End

DISTANCE 4 Miles   **TOWN** Egremont
DIFFICULTY RATING Moderate   **TRAIL STYLE** Loop
TRAIL TYPE Singletrack/Doubletrack

The loop trail at Jug End State Reservation in the South Taconic Range offers scenic striding across open fields, through mixed woodlands and forests, and along a deep stream gorge. The lower end is at the site of a former hotel and ski resort, abandoned decades ago, called Jug End Barn. Jug End is also the name of the northernmost peak on the mountain ridge above. The route described here leads from the base of the valley up one side of Fenton Brook and down the other. The forested portions are marked with blue blazes (plastic triangles with a picture of an acorn) and the field portions are mowed. Note that there is no longer a maintained trail connecting this loop to the Appalachian Trail (AT) or Jug End peak on the ridge above.

DIRECTIONS From Rte. 7 in Great Barrington, drive west on Rte. 23/41 for 4 miles. At Mill Pond, turn left on Rte. 41 south. In 0.1 miles, just past the pond, turn right on Mt. Washington Road and go west for 1.7 miles to a left turn onto Jug End Road. Go south for 0.5 miles and turn right into a large dirt parking area.

TRAIL Starting at the parking area, follow the line of stones right (west) on the Jug End Loop Trail. It immediately crosses Fenton Brook on a wide wooden bridge and then turns left (south). For the next 0.5 miles or so, the trail undulates across a meadow. At a junction, you could take the left fork for the most direct route to the rest of the loop. Instead, take a right here and follow the mowed path across the meadow. This is a great place to slow

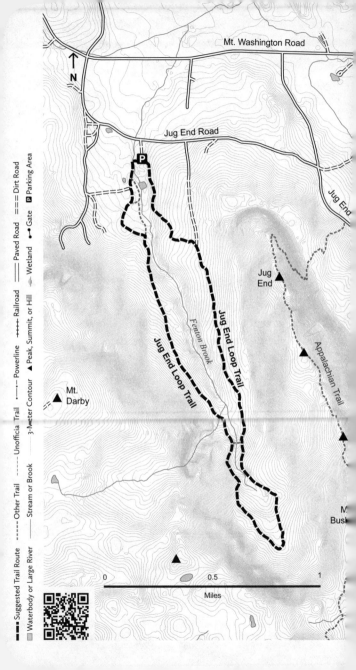

Open field portion of the Jug End Loop Trail.

down for a moment and look for wildflowers and wildlife. Stay left at a junction with an old road that leads right (west) toward a residential area, then pass a junction with a short link path on the left. At the next junction, go straight (south) and enter the woods.

Here, the trail begins to climb along an old road. Bear left where an overgrown road leads right. The grade is moderate for most of the way, but there are occasional steeper pitches and several eroded sections at crossings of rocky tributary streams. The roadway may be muddy here after heavy rains.

About 1 mile up from the meadow, you reach the stone chimney of a former cabin. A trail leads left here and crosses the brook to a junction with the Loop Trail on the far side, offering a potentially shorter route. Take the trail uphill to the right of the cabin. Heading south, this narrower trail climbs steeply for a short distance, then levels off and traverses the slope. Near the head of the valley, it passes above a rustic old cabin and crosses the headwaters of Fenton Brook. Old United States Geological Survey topo maps show a connector trail up to the AT on the ridge from here, but at present it appears to be overgrown and reclaimed by the forest. Circling tightly left, the trail now descends northward along the eastern side of the brook. Portions of the trail may be wet here.

After reaching the junction where the link trail leads left, continue straight. Cross another wet area, this time on a series of wooden boardwalks, then emerge at the first of several mown meadows with excellent views north and west to the peaks of Mt. Darby, Mt. Sterling, and Mt. Whitbeck. The trail skirts the upper edges of the meadows, then re-enters the woods on the lower end. Descend past an old spruce plantation and through an overgrown orchard and onto an old woods road. Finish the loop by turning left off the road to drop down a steep but short grassy path to the parking area.

NEARBY Just 1.2 miles east, take the AT steeply west up the ridge from Jug End Road for about 0.75 miles to the view from ledges on Jug End; continue south another 1 mile along the ridge to Mt. Bushnell, 2 miles to Guilder Pond, or 3 miles to the summit of Mt. Everett.

Alander Mountain

DISTANCE 8 Miles **TOWNS** Egremont/Mt. Washington
DIFFICULTY RATING Moderate/Challenging
TRAIL STYLE Loop/Out-and-Back
TRAIL TYPE Singletrack/Doubletrack/Dirt Road

The view southwest into New York from the open ridge of Alander Mountain should rank very high on any list of the most scenic mountain views in Massachusetts. At only 2,239 ft., the summit is quite low for such a panoramic vista, and it is not especially difficult to reach the top. A run can be done as a 5-mile out-and-back trip or turned into a longer loop run, as described here.

DIRECTIONS From Rte. 7 in Great Barrington, drive west on Rte. 23/41 for 4 miles. At Mill Pond, turn left on Rte. 41 south. In 0.1 miles, just past the pond, turn right on Mt. Washington Road (which becomes East Street) and go first west, then south for 9 miles to the Mt. Washington State Forest headquarters, just past an intersection with West Street. The driveway curves right and ends at a large dirt parking area.

TRAIL Starting at the trailhead, follow Alander Mountain Trail west for 0.5 miles through a series of open fields and woodlands to Lee Pond Brook, which the trail crosses on a sturdy wooden bridge. The trail then follows an old road, passing junctions on the left with the Charcoal Pit and Ashley Hill Trails, one of which you may eventually use on your return journey.

The Alander Mountain Trail then descends to Ashley Hill Brook, which it crosses on another wooden bridge. Keep following this trail west, traversing the slope and ascending gently. In 0.8 miles, you pass a junction with an unnamed trail that

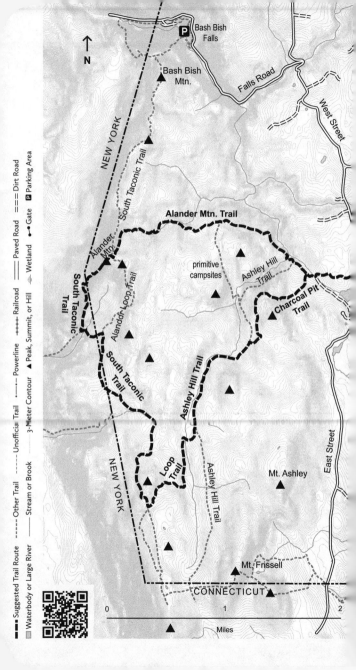

N

Bash Bish Falls

Bash Bish Mtn.

Falls Road

West Street

NEW YORK

South Taconic Trail

Alander Mtn. Trail

Alander Mtn.

primitive campsites

Ashley Hill Trail

South Taconic Trail

Alander Loop Trail

Charcoal Pit Trail

Ashley Hill Trail

South Taconic Trail

Ashley Hill Trail

East Street

Loop Trail

Ashley Hill Trail

Mt. Ashley

NEW YORK

Mt. Frissell

CONNECTICUT

Suggested Trail Route ---- Other Trail ----- Unofficial Trail === Dirt Road
—— Paved Road — Railroad ---- Powerline ● Gate 🅿 Parking Area
Wetland --- 3-Meter Contour —— Stream or Brook
Waterbody or Large River

0   1   2

Miles

leads left to backcountry campsites. Stay straight and keep going west. At first the trail traverses the slope at a very runnable grade, then it climbs more steeply, narrowing and getting a little rougher as it goes. Eventually, a little over 1 mile from the previous junction, you come to a cabin in the woods just below the crest of the Taconic Ridge.

At a somewhat confusing trail junction just beyond the cabin (where a similarly named but different trail called the Alander Loop Trail actually descends to the south), take a right on Alander Mountain Trail and climb steeply up a series of ledges to the crest of the Taconic Ridge. Then, at a junction with the South Taconic Trail, take a left and go a short distance south to the summit of Alander Mountain.

After taking in the expansive view, continue your run by following South Taconic Trail southwest. The next 0.25 miles of fully exposed, wide-open ridge running is simply epic. The trail then crosses the state line and veers slightly left (south), dropping steeply back down into the forest. At 0.8 miles from the summit, it reaches a 3-way junction with Alander Brook Trail. Take a left and continue on the wide South Taconic Trail, bearing southeast back into Massachusetts.

After passing a junction with the lower end of Alander Loop Trail, via which you could potentially shorten your run into a 7-mile lollipop route, follow South Taconic Trail for another 2 miles south. The footing is generally quite good, and the grade is never steep. Along the way you pass junctions on the right with Robert Brook Trail and an alternate spur path. The spur path leads to some views from a semi-open area and then continues on, reconnecting to South Taconic Trail shortly afterwards. At a junction with the Loop Trail, turn left and head northeast.

The Loop Trail is the roughest part of this route. It is only lightly used, and it can be wet and overgrown in places. After a mile of descending, it crosses Ashley Hill Brook and meets up with the more frequently traveled Ashley Hill Trail.

OPTIONAL EXTENSION An extra mile of running south on South Taconic Trail will take you briefly into Connecticut and bring you to the southern end of Ashley Hill Trail, eliminating the Loop Trail portion of the described route and lengthening the run by 1.5 miles.

From the junction with Loop Trail, descend along Ashley Hill Trail for 1 mile to a junction. Here, you can either take Charcoal Pit Trail up and then back down to Alander Mountain Trail, or simply keep going north down Ashley Hill Trail, which also connects with Alander Mountain Trail. The Charcoal Pit Trail has some nice gentle sections, but it also has a few rough ones marked by gnarly roots and wet areas to cross. Whichever way you choose, head east once you reach Alander Mountain Trail and return to the parking area to complete your run.

NEARBY From the summit of Alander Mountain, the South Taconic Trail leads 2 miles north to Bash Bish Mountain, from which a 2-mile loop trail descends to Bash Bish Falls State Park.

DISTANCE 3.5 Miles **TOWN** Granville
DIFFICULTY RATING Easy/Moderate **TRAIL STYLE** Loop
TRAIL TYPE Singletrack/Doubletrack

Granville State Forest in the southeastern Berkshires offers miles of scenic trails along streams, past cascades, and through both dark hemlock groves and brighter hardwood stands. The short loop run described here combines several singletrack trails, some narrow doubletrack, and a short section of dirt road. There are several possible extensions, and one option that includes a shallow stream crossing of the Hubbard River.

DIRECTIONS From Rte. 189 in the village of Granville, go 6 miles west on Rte. 56. Turn left onto West Hartland Road and go 1 mile south down to a bridge over the Hubbard River. The large dirt parking area is on the left just past the bridge.

TRAIL From the parking area, go right (east) on West Hartland Road. Immediately turn right again onto a paved lane, pass a metal gate, and follow the lane south into the woods. This mossy road parallels the Hubbard River, which descends alongside to the left. In about 0.5 miles you arrive at a bulb at the end of the paved section of road. A short spur path leads left here to a beautiful view of a waterfall along the river.

From the bulb, the trail continues south over mostly level ground and very soon reaches a junction where the Camp Trail leads right (west) up to the campground. Stay straight (south). The trail soon passes a scenic cascade along Halfway Brook on the right, then crosses Halfway Brook and reaches a junction with Halfway Brook Trail. Left leads down to a utility crossing of the Hubbard River, but go right and follow Halfway Brook Trail west as it gradually climbs beneath conifers along the southern bank of Halfway Brook. In 0.5 miles, the trail reaches a picnic area next to West Hartland Road just south of the campground.

Optional Extension To add an extra half mile to your run, cross the road and take the Beaver Pond Loop trail, going straight (west) and looping around until you reach a junction with the Sattler Trail. Be sure to go left (north) to complete the loop. This mostly level trail has nice, soft footing, and there is a partial view out across a marsh.

Go north on West Hartland Road for 0.1 miles, passing the trailhead for the Ordway Trail across from the campground entrance, then bear left into the woods on the CCC Trail (named for the Civilian Conservation Corps). This somewhat overgrown doubletrack trail climbs gently at first and then follows relatively level ground around a forested swamp. In about 0.2 miles, pass two junctions with the HQ Trail on the right. About 0.7 miles from the road, turn right (east) at a junction with the Corduroy Trail. This wide trail crosses the forested swamp and may be soggy at its lowest point. At a junction with the HQ Trail, go left and follow the grassy road a short distance around a curve to West Hartland Road. Go left on the road, running level at first and then steeply downhill, for 0.5 miles back to the parking lot.

Alternate Option This route is similar to the one described, but the beginning parallels the other side of the Hubbard River and requires a shallow stream crossing after about a mile. From the parking area, go right on West Hartland Road. Cross the bridge over the river and turn right onto the somewhat mossy paved road. Cross a washed-out portion on small bridges to the left. About 0.5 miles from West Hartland Road, the road ends at a turnaround. The Hubbard River Trail veers left off the road here

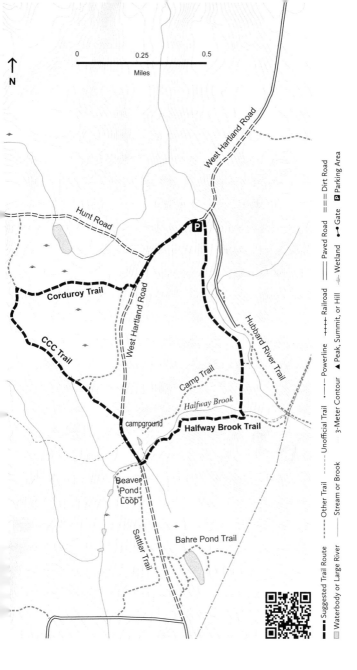

0   0.25   0.5

Miles

N

West Hartland Road

Hunt Road

Corduroy Trail

CCC Trail

West Hartland Road

Hubbard River Trail

Camp Trail

Halfway Brook

campground

Halfway Brook Trail

Beaver
Pond
Loop

Sattler Trail

Bahre Pond Trail

Suggested Trail Route ---- Other Trail ..... Unofficial Trail +++ Railroad ---- Powerline ▲ Peak, Summit, or Hill 🅿 Parking Area
Waterbody or Large River ── Stream or Brook ── Paved Road === Dirt Road ⊸ Gate ⎶ Wetland ── 3-Meter Contour

and becomes rugged singletrack. Passing mostly beneath dark conifers, you soon reach an unmarked spur trail that leads off to the right to a view of the waterfall. From that junction, the trail continues south, descending to a powerline crossing about 1 mile south of West Hartland Road. If the current isn't too strong or the flow too high, cross the river and meet up with the lower end of Halfway Brook Trail on the other side.

NEARBY Nice loops can be run on the Gilmore and Farmington River Trails at Tolland State Forest, about 8 miles to the northwest in Tolland. Bonus: swim in Otis Reservoir afterward!

DISTANCE 4 Miles   TOWNS Chester/Blandford

DIFFICULTY RATING Moderate/Challenging

TRAIL STYLE Loop   TRAIL TYPE Singletrack/Doubletrack/Dirt Road

This moderately challenging loop run at Chester-Blandford State Forest covers a wide variety of terrain and trail types. It passes close to a spectacular waterfall and features a sweeping view across the Westfield River valley. The distance, elevation gain, steepness, and occasionally rough footing place it in the challenging category, but overall it is a very pleasant run. Additionally, the brook itself has several nice pools along Sanderson Brook Road that make nice spots to cool off after a hot summer run.

DIRECTIONS From Westfield, take Rte. 20 west for about 16 miles to the large dirt parking area at Sanderson Brook Road in Chester, passing by two other Chester-Blandford State Forest signs on the left. From Lee, take Rte. 20 east for about 20 miles to the parking area on the right.

TRAIL Starting at the parking area on the south side of Rte. 20, head south up Sanderson Brook Road. This is an unpaved woods road, though it is well maintained and the footing is generally good. After passing through a closed metal gate and crossing a metal bridge over Sanderson Brook, the trail soon arrives at a junction with the H. Newman Marsh Memorial Trail, a singletrack trail leading up the slope to the left that you will eventually come down at the end of your run.

    Continuing straight, the road ascends gradually along Sanderson Brook. It crosses the brook on bridges two more times; there are no railings on these bridges and they're just high

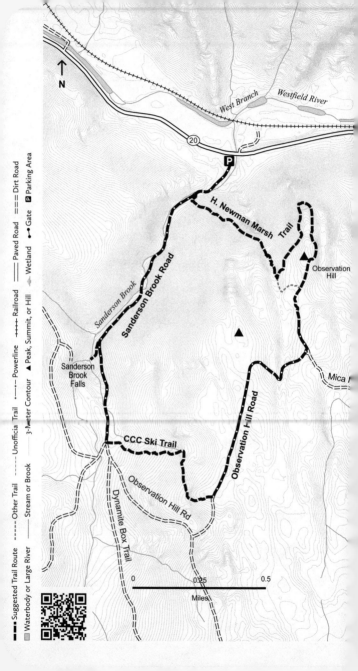

enough that a fall would be dangerous, so make sure to stay safe on them. About 0.9 miles from the start, go right on a narrow trail leading down the slope toward the brook on the right. This is a short side trail to Sanderson Brook Falls, a 60-foot-high cascade that can be extremely impressive in the spring or after heavy rains. From the falls, take the spur trail back out to the road.

Bearing right from the spur trail, the road begins to climb more steeply along a section where the roadbed is made up of slightly coarser rocks that can be uncomfortable underfoot. In about 0.25 miles, it levels out and arrives at an intersection.

Alternate Option For an easier climb than the following section describes, you could continue straight on the road, which becomes Beulah Land Road, and almost immediately veer left at the next fork. Then ascend for 0.5 miles to another intersection and turn left on Observation Hill Road.

Take a left onto an unmarked route called the CCC Ski Trail, which ascends the mountainside very steeply through a dark conifer forest for about 0.25 miles before leveling out and climbing for another 0.25 miles at a gentler grade. It ends at a junction with Observation Hill Road. The lower part of the trail is eroded in places and can be fairly rough and wet, but the footing gets better the higher you go, and the upper part where it emerges into a lighter and drier hardwood forest is quite runnable.

At the intersection with Observation Hill Road, turn left and run along the broad ridge for about 0.5 miles. The road gently rises and falls along this section, generally sticking to high ground but occasionally crossing over wet swales and saddles. Then it turns right and drops at a steady but not-too-steep grade down some switchbacks for 0.25 miles to a triangle junction with Mica Mine Road. Take a left here and go 0.2 miles to a bulb at the end of the dirt road. Here, the blue-blazed H. Newman Marsh Memorial Trail heads north into the woods. In about

Sanderson Brook Falls at Chester-Blandford State Forest in Chester.

0.1 miles, it passes a junction with a now-closed trail, then continues straight and passes by several limited views along the east side of Observation Hill. Descending slightly, the trail eventually arrives at a spectacular open ledge with a view of the forested valley to the northwest.

From the vista, the trail swings left and then traverses south along the west side of Observation Hill. Take care to make a hard right at a hairpin turn just before the trail reaches a brook; the closed but still-blazed connector trail leads left up the hill here. Descend the slope northwest for a short way, sometimes steeply, then take a left and cross the stream. The trail briefly descends along the left side of the stream, then veers left and continues downslope to a junction with Sanderson Brook Road. Turn right here and follow the road back to the parking area.

NEARBY Run a scenic 3-mile loop along the network of trails at the Becket Land Trust Historic Quarry and Forest, located about 6 miles west in the towns of Becket and Otis.

DISTANCE 5 Miles   TOWN Chester/Middlefield
DIFFICULTY RATING Easy/Moderate   TRAIL STYLE Out-and-Back
TRAIL TYPE Singletrack/Doubletrack/Dirt Road

The Keystone Arch Bridges Trail (KAB Trail) combines a variety of trail types and difficulties and offers a bounty of both natural and historical scenery. Mostly following the bed of a discontinued roadway, it passes several large, arched stone bridges over the West Branch of the Westfield River as well as numerous cascades, quarries, and old foundations. There are several jeep trails and old roads intersecting along the way, but the route is easy to follow, with occasional blue paint blazes and rectangular KAB Trail markers tacked (often high up) onto trees. This trail makes a very fun run that provides more of a challenge than a typical rail trail. The out-and-back distance is about five miles, but short side trips out to the various bridges, which are well worth a look, will raise the mileage slightly.

DIRECTIONS From Rte. 20 in Chester, follow Middlefield Road northwest for 2.5 miles to where the road begins to climb to the north. The unpaved Herbert Cross Road will be on the left, though the sign may be missing. There is parking here for several vehicles. Take care when pulling off of Middlefield Road as the pavement lip is fairly steep and low-clearance vehicles may scrape. There is a trailhead sign here, with a map of the route.

TRAIL Starting at Middlefield Road, the trail follows a dirt road (Herbert Cross Road) down a short hill and crosses a stream on a metal grate bridge. To the right, a small but scenic waterfall cascades down the rocky streambed. To the left, the first of the keystone arch bridges can be seen just downstream. There is no official trail leading to the riverbank, but it's easy enough to poke your way down for a good view. This bridge, Keystone Bridge E, is an impressive double-arch structure that is still in use as an active rail line, and you may see passenger or cargo trains crossing it.

Continuing along the road, the trail follows the north bank of the river. In about 1,000 feet, it swings left at a sharp bend in the river where there is a good view upstream to the next bridge. Passing a junction where a road leads upslope to the right, follow trail markers to the left and arrive at another junction. The trail bears right here, but you can take a quick side trip straight ahead to look at the next bridge, an iron-girder deck bridge that is still in use. Back at the junction, go up the main road as it turns right and gradually ascends a gentle slope. Soon, the trail turns right off the road, passes through an old stone wall, and narrows to singletrack for about a mile.

The trail gradually climbs the hillside, then traverses west along it. At a junction in the woods where several unmarked trails split off, a wooden kiosk provides site information and a trail map. From here, keep following the trail markers slightly to the left. The trail soon veers into a drainage ravine and crosses a scenic stream on a pedestrian bridge. Then it descends the slope back to the old road (from here, it is possible to take another out-and-back side trip to Keystone Bridge C by going left along the road for a few hundred feet). Bearing right, the trail rejoins the road and continues southwest.

The trail, now following the old route of the Pontoosic Turnpike, soon arrives at a junction next to Keystone Bridge B, where a short side trip will lead you out onto the top of the huge stone structure. Be extremely careful here as there are no railings and it's a long way down to the river. Just before the bridge, the trail turns right and heads west above the north bank of the river,

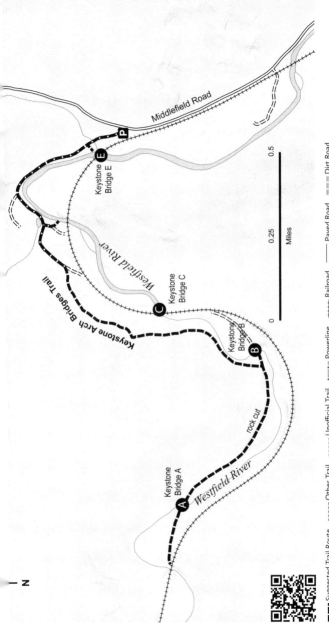

N

Middlefield Road

0.5

0.25

0

Miles

P Parking Area

Keystone
Bridge E

Westfield River

Keystone
Bridge C

Keystone Arch Bridges Trail

Keystone
Bridge B

rock cut

Keystone
Bridge A

Westfield River

— ■ — Suggested Trail Route   ----- Other Trail   ······ Powerline   —— Paved Road   === Dirt Road
▨ Waterbody or Large River   —— Stream or Brook   ----- Unofficial Trail   +++++ Railroad   ⟿ Wetland   •— Gate

3-Meter Contour   ▲ Peak, Summit, or Hill

soon passing a view across the gorge below. Continue straight over level ground, passing by a quarry site and through a deep road cut with cliff walls on either side. The ground may be wet in the road cut.

The trail soon arrives at Keystone Bridge A, another now-abandoned stone bridge over the river. It then continues west for about 0.25 miles and ends at the active rail lines. Be careful when approaching the tracks since trains can come by at any time. Here, turn around and retrace your route back to the trailhead.

NEARBY About 6 miles to the south, the Becket Land Trust Historic Quarry and Forest in Becket features miles of scenic trails.

Chesterfield Gorge
(East Branch Trail)

DISTANCE 15–18 Miles **TOWNS** Chesterfield/Huntington

DIFFICULTY RATING Easy **TRAIL STYLE** Out-and-Back

TRAIL TYPE Doubletrack

SITE DESCRIPTION On its journey south toward the Connecticut River, the East Branch of the Westfield River flows though Chesterfield Gorge, a narrow chasm of bedrock. Lacking any current development, this stretch of the Westfield is designated as a National Wild and Scenic River. The East Branch Trail, also called River Road, is an old dirt road that parallels the river along its western bank for 9 miles from the gorge to the Knightville Dam in Huntington. There are marker posts at each mile. The trail passes through multiple conservation lands, though most of it falls within Gilbert A. Bliss State Forest and the federally owned Knightville Wildlife Management Area. In places the road is somewhat eroded into ruts and rough patches, and there are occasional small stream crossings and wet spots, but overall this is a relatively easy run without any major turns to be concerned about. Designated as multiple-use, River Road is sometimes used by ATV and dirt bike riders. An alternate way to do this run is to park along Rte. 112 just north of the dam and head north.

DIRECTIONS The northern parking area for this trail is located about 3.5 miles west of Chesterfield. From the center of town in Chesterfield, head west on Rte. 143 down the big hill for about 2 miles and cross the Westfield River at the bottom, then turn south on Ireland Street. Go south for 0.8 mile on Ireland Street, then turn left onto River Road, following signs for Chesterfield Gorge. Go about 0.5 miles to the parking area for The Trustees

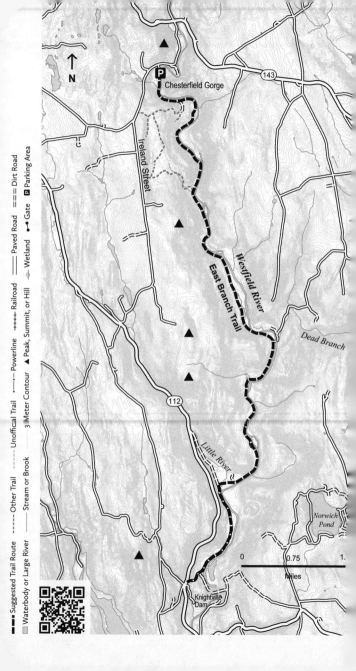

Legend

- ■ ■ ■ Suggested Trail Route
- ■■■■ Waterbody or Large River
- ---- Other Trail
- ----- Unofficial Trail
- ······ Powerline
- ╪╪╪ Railroad
- ── Stream or Brook
- ── Paved Road
- ═══ Dirt Road
- ▬ Wetland
- ▲ Peak, Summit, or Hill
- — 3 Meter Contour
- P Parking Area
- ◆ Gate

N

Chesterfield Gorge

143

Ireland Street

Westfield River

East Branch Trail

Dead Branch

112

Little River

Norwich Pond

0   0.75   1.

Miles

Knightville Dam

of Reservations (TTOR) Chesterfield Gorge property. In season, TTOR may charge a small fee to nonmembers seeking to park here, and donations are encouraged when no attendant is present. Parking is also available slightly farther down on River Road at a private lot owned by a local snowmobile club, where a small donation is also requested. Coming from the west, head east down the hill on Rte. 143 from the center of Worthington for 5 miles to Ireland Street. From the south, go north from Rte. 20 in Huntington for 9 miles to Ireland Street, then take Ireland Street north about 4 miles to River Road and take a right.

TRAIL A short path starting at the TTOR parking area follows the upper edge of Chesterfield Gorge at the northern end. It's not really an appropriate trail for running, but the scenic chasm is certainly worth checking out before or after your run.

Follow River Road south down the hill for several hundred feet to the bank of the river. There is direct access to the river itself here, with nice views both upstream and downstream; this spot makes a nice place to cool off near the end of a long run on a hot summer day. Continuing south, the road enters Chesterfield Gorge State Forest (formerly East Branch State Forest). Look for a pretty cascade along a small stream on the right. A mile from the start, the road rises, veers slightly inland, and passes through a dark, conifer-dominated area with several large boulders. At 1.5 miles, the road becomes sandy for a stretch but the footing is still good. At around 2 miles, the road passes through a gate.

At 3.0 miles from the start, part of the foundation of an old mill is visible near a bend in the river. For the next few miles, the road continues south, gently rising and falling over varied terrain. Several smaller side trails lead steeply off to the right, and two more metal gates are passed. At 5.0 miles, the trail arrives at the first of several cleared fields. At about 6.8 miles, it leaves the woods for good and enters an open marshy area created by high water levels in Knightville Reservoir, part of a large Army Corps of Engineers flood control project. Somewhere along this section the name technically changes to Army Corps of Engineers Road. At 7.6 miles, the road crosses a concrete bridge over Little River (flowing in from the right), after which the surface briefly changes to pavement. At 7.7 miles, it reaches a junction with Old Worthington Road. For the 15-mile run, turn back here and end just before re-climbing the final hill to the parking lot.

For the longest option, turn left just south of the concrete bridge and run south for 1.5 miles along the road through a treeless floodplain to the next junction, at 9.0 miles (this section can be quite warm on a hot summer day, so make sure you've brought enough water). Just before the road begins climbing the hill, it forks. Stay straight and go 0.3 miles up to a junction with Rte. 112. The return trip is slightly uphill but the elevation gain is barely noticeable.

NEARBY About 12 miles west, the Dorothy Frances Rice Wildlife Sanctuary in Peru features several miles of moderately challenging scenic trails.

DISTANCE 7.5 Miles **TOWNS** Goshen/Ashfield
DIFFICULTY RATING Moderate
TRAIL STYLE Loop **TRAIL TYPE** Singletrack

Daughters of the American Revolution (DAR) State Forest in Goshen and Ashfield features nearly 20 miles of trails and old roads, many of which are excellent for running. The run described here utilizes mostly singletrack hiking and mountain bike trails, but many other interesting options and variations are possible. Most of the route is dry, though there are some occasional wet areas, such as on the far side of the Hootenanny Loop and along the edge of Upper Highland Lake. The trails are inconsistently blazed (with at least three different colors on the same trail sometimes), particularly along the optional extensions, so care should be taken to study the map and orient yourself as you go. The trail network currently connects to trails at The Trustees of Reservations' (TTOR) Chapel Brook and Bullitt Reservations to the northeast via the 2.5-mile Chapel Brook to DAR Trail, and a much longer and very nice trail run can be cobbled together by combining the sites.

DIRECTIONS From Northampton, take Rte. 9 west for about 13 miles to Goshen. Then go north on Rte. 112 for almost a mile to the DAR State Forest access road on the right. From the fee station at the entrance, go 0.5 miles east and then turn left at a sign for the boat ramp and campground. A large paved parking lot is located immediately to the right.

TRAIL Starting at the parking area, go back out to the main paved road (Moore Hill Road), go left (east), and pass a gate for an unpaved road on the right. After a quick curve in the road, the trailhead is on the right, about 0.25 miles from the parking area. Immediately after entering the woods, turn left on the singletrack NEMBA Trail (named for the New England Mountain Bike Association) and follow it up the hill.

Optional Extension Instead of taking the NEMBA Trail, go south on Turkey Trail and make left turns on Town Trail and Black Bear Trail. This will take you over rougher terrain and bring you to the summit of Moore Hill. An additional possible extension on this route is an out-and-back spur to Balancing Rock, a large glacial erratic boulder.

From Moore Hill Road, NEMBA Trail weaves up Moore Hill via several long, gentle switchbacks. Near the top, the trail splits briefly—here, the left fork traverses a set of semi-open rock ledges—but the two paths re-converge shortly thereafter. After leveling off, NEMBA Trail arrives at a 3-way trail junction next to a dirt road. Go left here and follow the road up to the fire tower at the 1,697-ft. summit of Moore Hill. On a clear day, the view from the tower encompasses a large swath of western Massachusetts, from Mt. Greylock in the west to Mt. Tom and the Holyoke Range in the east.

Optional Extension From the 3-way junction, follow Pine Marten Trail about 0.25 miles down the south side of the hill to a very large boulder sitting in a clearing in the woods, then return to the summit making about a half-mile out-and-back extension.

At the base of the tower, two trails lead north. The trail on the left follows a small powerline and leads directly back to the campground area; this is a good bail-out option if you need to cut your run short. To continue the run, take the trail on the right and descend the mountain, steeply at first. After curving right and passing junctions with the upper and lower ends of a slightly longer and narrower alternate trail on the left, the trail first crosses over a dirt access road and then turns left and crosses the paved Moore Hill Road. Now called the Long Trail,

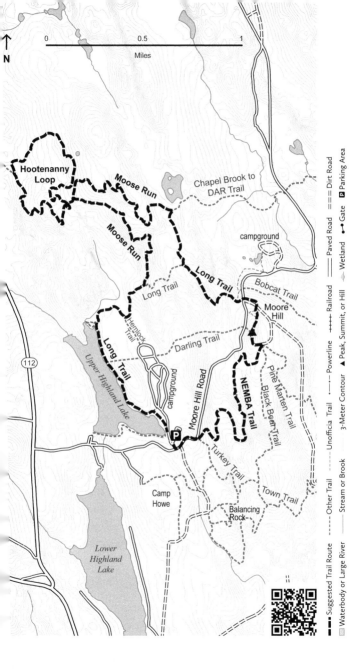

the trail heads north about 0.5 miles to a 3-way junction with the Moose Run loop trail.

Optional Trim It is possible to go left here and descend the Long Trail for a much shorter version of this loop.

Take a right and immediately cross over a stone wall, then continue north to another 3-way junction. Take a sharp left and continue on the Moose Run loop, now heading west. The trail climbs slightly through conifers and then undulates across a hardwood-dominated upland where the dense understory of ferns is truly remarkable. The trail descends to a junction with the Hootenanny Loop near a stone wall. Take this short spur to a newly constructed, 1.7-mile loop trail. Following the loop clockwise, the trail gradually descends to a junction just east of Rte. 112. A spur leads left (northwest) to a private driveway off of Rte. 112 (there is no parking here). Take a right and follow the north half of the Hootenanny Loop back around to the junction, then take a left on the spur and head back to the Moose Run loop. Go right and follow Moose Run, rising and falling as you gradually ascend to the southeast.

At a junction with the Long Trail, go right and descend to a set of wooden bridges that cross a small swamp. Pass Hemlock Trail on the left (leading up [south] to the campground), and continue heading generally southwest. Soon you arrive at the northeastern shore of Upper Highland Lake. Now follow the Long Trail south through mountain laurel thickets along the lake's eastern shore, passing on the left the unmarked Fisher Trail (leading up [east] to the campground), and on the right the campground's lakefront swimming area. Eventually you come out at the campground access road, which you take back to the parking area.

NEARBY TTOR's Chapel Brook and Bullitt Reservation trails are accessible from this property via the 2.5-mile long and very runnable Chapel Brook to DAR connector trail.

DISTANCE 5 Miles **TOWN** Ashfield **DIFFICULTY RATING** Moderate
TRAIL STYLE Out-and-Back/Lollipop Loop **TRAIL TYPE** Singletrack

The Two Bridges Trail connects two properties owned by The Trustees of Reservations (TTOR) and the Chapel Brook and Bullitt Reservations. It features a fantastic diversity of natural features to enjoy, including a spectacular waterfall right near the road, miles of very nice trails, a huge glacial erratic boulder, and scenic views from open fields. The trail is a lollipop loop, with most of the route consisting of an out-and-back on the "stick" part. There are ups and downs along the way, but overall it's very runnable. It has only one short section steep enough that you will probably need to hike (or at least slow way down) to ascend but it is nicely constructed with a series of zig-zag switchbacks. In general, this well-marked, easy-to-follow trail is exceptionally pleasant for trail running.

DIRECTIONS To reach the southern parking area for this trail, take North Street about 7 miles north from Rte. 9 in Williamsburg. North Street becomes Ashfield Road and then Williamsburg Road. The main parking area is on the left (west) side of the road, next a sign for Chapel Brook Reservation, but limited parking is also available across the street at the start of the now-closed Chapel Falls Road. Together, the two areas can accommodate about 8 vehicles. The northern parking area is at the Bullitt Reservation, about a mile south of Rte. 116 on Bullitt Road in Ashfield.

TRAIL Beginning at the Two Bridges Trail trailhead on the east side of Williamsburg Road, the trail descends for about 0.25 miles along Chapel Falls Road, passing several spur trails down to Chapel Falls on the left within the first 0.1 miles. At a sign-

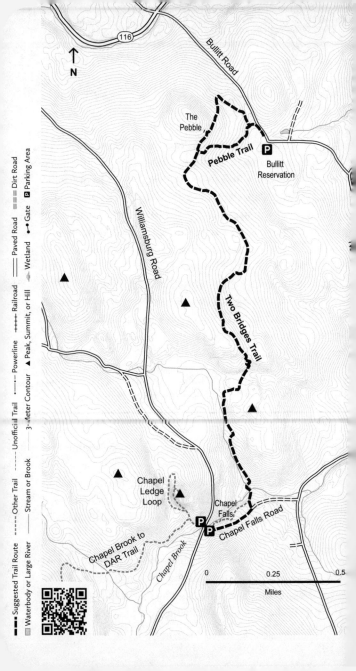

116

Bullitt Road

The Pebble

Pebble Trail

P Bullitt Reservation

Williamsburg Road

Two Bridges Trail

Chapel Ledge Loop

P

Chapel Falls

Chapel Falls Road

Chapel Brook to DAR Trail

Chapel Brook

N

Suggested Trail Route
Waterbody or Large River
Other Trail
Unofficial Trail
Stream or Brook
Powerline
Railroad
Paved Road
Dirt Road
Wetland
Gate
Peak, Summit, or Hill
Parking Area

0   0.25   0.5

Miles

post, the trail veers left off the old road and becomes singletrack. It drops steeply down through the woods for another 0.25 miles to Chapel Brook, which it crosses via the namesake two bridges, each made of sturdy, heavy timbers that are clearly built to last.

From the bridges, the trail climbs gradually along a feeder brook for a while. Then it becomes steeper and climbs the slope via a series of nice switchbacks. At the top of the switchbacks, there's about a mile of easy running through the woods, rising and falling gently and occasionally passing by and through old stone walls. Eventually, the trail arrives at a marked junction that begins the loop portion of the run. As this is a fairly new trail at the time of this writing, small cut stumps can make footing a little tricky in places, but they will rot and smooth over in a few years.

Taking a left, the trail climbs and passes a big boulder (called "The Pebble") wedged among several trees and then drops to a scenic view at the top edge of a mown field. The trail descends the left side of the field, then veers hard right and traverses right through the middle of it. Soon it comes to a junction where a short spur path leads down and out to the northern trailhead at the Bullitt Reservation. Continuing around the loop, the trail climbs back to the junction at the top of the lollipop "stick." This section can be a bit brushy and hard to follow, with brambles growing out into the trail in places. Once back at the 3-way junction, take the left fork to head back toward Chapel Falls parking area. After re-crossing the second wooden bridge, go right on a narrow unmarked trail that leads to the base of the waterfalls along Chapel Brook.

NEARBY DAR State Forest is accessible from this property via the 2.5-mile-long and very runnable Chapel Brook to DAR connector trail, which begins across the street from Chapel Falls Road (and includes a short side loop option to a view atop Chapel Ledge).

Bear Swamp Reservation

DISTANCE 3 Miles **TOWN** Ashfield
DIFFICULTY RATING Moderate/Challenging
TRAIL STYLE Loop **TRAIL TYPE** Singletrack

Bear Swamp Reservation is a property owned and managed by The Trustees of Reservations (TTOR). The route described here incorporates mostly trails on that land, but it also includes portions of trail maintained by Ashfield Trails. The landscape is rugged, with many ponds, streams, and wetlands interlaced among irregular rocky ridges and forested hillsides.

DIRECTIONS From Rte. 112 in Ashfield, go 1.7 miles west on Hawley Road (passing Bear Swamp Road on the left) to the signed trailhead on the left. There is space for several vehicles.

TRAIL Starting at the trailhead kiosk, follow the trail 0.1 miles southwest up the hill. At a 3-way junction, go left on Beaver Brook Trail. You soon arrive at the eastern end of a pond. This is the closest you'll get to the water on this run. Continue south to another 3-way junction. Go left here on the Fern Glade Trail, which climbs gradually south up to a height of land and skirts the edge of some vernal pools. On the other side of the rise, it drops gently for about 0.5 miles to Bear Swamp Road.

> **OPTIONAL EXTENSION** To add 1.2 miles and a significant climb to your run, cross the road and go south on Peter Hill Trail. This trail is well maintained and the footing is good. Along the way, you'll cross a powerline and pass just below a private residence. The wooded top of 1,834-ft. Peter Hill is marked with a sign. From there, return north to resume the route.

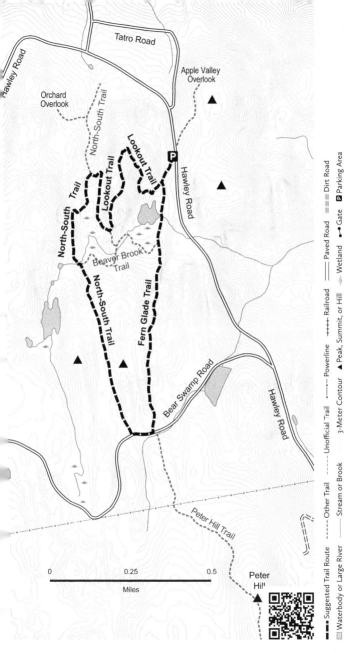

Tatro Road

Hawley Road

Apple Valley
Overlook

Orchard
Overlook

North-South Trail

Lookout Trail

Lookout Trail

North-South Trail

Hawley Road

Beaver Brook
Trail

North-South Trail

Fern Glade Trail

Bear Swamp Road

Hawley Road

Peter Hill Trail

0   0.25   0.5

Miles

Peter
Hill

▬ Suggested Trail Route   ----- Other Trail   ----- Unofficial Trail   ── Paved Road   +─+─+ Railroad   ═══ Dirt Road
▬ Waterbody or Large River   ── Stream or Brook   ── 3-Meter Contour   ▲ Peak, Summit, or Hill   •─• Gate   🅿 Parking Area

Go right (west) on Bear Swamp Road and find the start of the North-South Trail on the right, along a curve in the road. Take this trail north and ascend very gradually for about 0.5 miles. At a subtle height of land, the trail begins to descend and soon arrives at a 3-way junction close to a cascade along a small stream.

Optional Trim To shorten the run, go right here and descend along the Beaver Brook Trail. The trail follows the bank of a scenic woodland brook and soon arrives at a 3-way junction. Go right and descend a little further, then bear right, away from the stream and along the southern shore of the pond. Then, at another 3-way junction, go left and stay straight at the next junction to return back to the parking area.

Go left at the cascade and take the North-South Trail north along the edge of the property. A wetland is below to the right, and a managed forest is visible to the left. The trail drops to cross a stream and then continues north. At 0.3 miles from the cascade you arrive at a 3-way junction with the Lookout Trail.

Optional Extension This worthwhile out-and-back requires one short climb each way. Go left and descend at a moderate grade for 0.2 miles on the North-South Trail to a marked junction with a spur path up to a scenic vista at the upper edge of a private orchard. Go left on the spur path and climb about 0.1 miles to the lookout, then turn around at the Orchard Outlook.

Take a right on the Lookout Trail and climb gradually for a short distance. The trail makes a sharp turn south and passes between two ridges before swinging east and climbing again. At a 3-way junction, go left and scramble up to the top of a rocky ridge, where there is a limited view east across the pond. The trail then climbs north along this ridge to the top of a forested hill. Then it swings right and descends to near the northern edge of the pond. The footing is somewhat rough over the rugged terrain in this section. After crossing a low ridge and arriving back at the first 3-way junction, go left to return to the parking lot.

NEARBY From Peter Hill, the Sanderson Academy Trail continues south to Rte. 116 in Ashfield; the Ashfield Trails committee maintains this and other excellent trails in town.

DISTANCE 13 Miles   TOWNS Deerfield/Shelburne
DIFFICULTY RATING Easy/Moderate/Challenging
TRAIL STYLE Out-and-Back   TRAIL TYPE Singletrack/Doubletrack

The Mahican-Mohawk (M/M) Trail, not to be confused with the region's *other* double-M long-distance trail, the Metacomet-Monadnock (M-M) Trail, runs west from the Connecticut River valley to the New York state line. It is still in the process of being completed. The section described here links Deerfield to Shelburne. It gets progressively more technical as you go west, and ultimately ends at a waterfall just before a closed section. A combination of round Mahican-Mohawk trail markers and white blazes are used to mark the route the whole way.

DIRECTIONS From Deerfield village, go south about 2 miles on Mill Village Road. Take a right onto Stillwater Road and go 1.4 miles. Turn right onto Hoosac Road and go 0.25 miles. Park at the trailhead on the right, where there is space for about four vehicles, and make sure to not block the road.

TRAIL Start at the parking area and follow the trail, which coincides with a dirt road, for about 0.15 miles between two fields. Then, at a gate with some signage, continue straight along the road for another 0.2 miles to the first of three alternate single-track routes that branch off to the right. This first branch is arguably the least interesting, but all are worth taking for variety.

The first alternate branch (loop 1) leads right and crosses a powerline swath, then dips into the woods on the other side. The trail is easy to follow and fairly gentle. It rejoins the main trail in 0.3 miles. After a brief stint back on the main trail, the

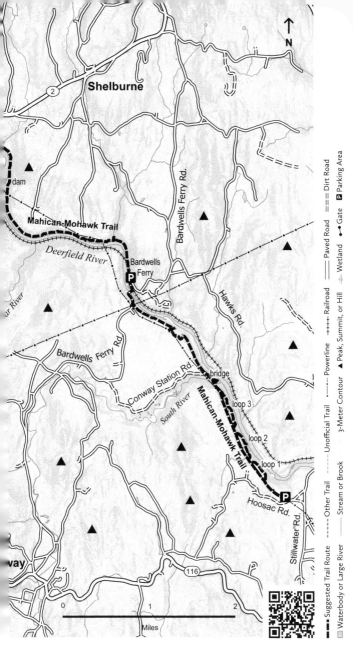

↑
N

Shelburne

2

dam

Mahican-Mohawk Trail

Deerfield River

Bardwells Ferry Rd.

Bardwells
Ferry

P

Hawks Rd.

ar River

Bardwells Ferry Rd.

Conway Station Rd.

bridge

South River

Mahican-Mohawk Trail

loop 3

loop 2

loop 1

P

Hoosac Rd.

Stillwater Rd.

ay

116

0   1   2
Miles

Suggested Trail Route   ----- Other Trail   ----- Unofficial Trail   ===== Dirt Road

Waterbody or Large River   — Stream or Brook   — 3-Meter Contour   — Paved Road   +++ Railroad   ···· Powerline   ▲ Peak, Summit, or Hill   —• Gate   P Parking Area second branch (loop 2) splits off to the right. This branch is slightly longer and has more ups and downs. It rejoins the main trail in 0.4 miles. After another brief stretch on the main trail, the third branch (loop 3) splits off to the right. This branch is the longest and most challenging of the loops, with many ups and downs. It rejoins the main trail in 0.5 miles, at the top of a bluff.

The trail then descends very steeply for 0.1 miles down to a pedestrian bridge called Polly's Crossing over the mouth of the South River. The soil can be loose here, so be careful if you decide to run down it. Across the bridge, the trail turns right, then left, then climbs the steep bluff on the other side. At the top, continue along the now-wider trail through a turnaround at the end of Conway Station Road. Soon, the otherwise straight and flat trail reaches a section where the old roadbed has eroded away, and it dips down to the left to cross a narrow earthen bridge next to a small cascade. On the other side, the trail continues along the old roadbed. In 0.25 miles, the trail veers left up into the woods at a wet spot to avoid a section beyond which the roadbed has completely washed away. In 0.1 miles, after reaching and briefly following a powerline, the trail rejoins the roadbed on the other side of the washout. Continue for another 0.6 miles until the trail reaches a clearing just below Bardwells Ferry Road.

Climb up the steps to the paved road, then go right and follow it around a curve down the hill. Cross the Deerfield River on an iron bridge, curve left, and keep following the road to the first sharp turn. Look for the white blazes leading into the woods. There is parking here if you prefer to access the trail in the middle rather than the eastern end. Next, follow the trail to a set of active railroad tracks and cross them just before they traverse a bridge over the river.

The next section of trail is more rugged than the rest. It drops steeply down to a bend in the river, then rises and falls along the eastern shore of the river for about 3 miles. It crosses over several major tributary streams, passes beneath a few power-lines, and reaches a dam where there is a canoe portage path leading down to the water on the left. After the dam, the trail climbs away from the river for a while, then traverses a section of steep, wet slope on boardwalks. Eventually it arrives at a tributary stream in a hemlock ravine where cascades tumble down to the river below. At present, the trail ends here due to the request of a landowner.

NEARBY Moderately difficult out-and-back or loop runs can be done along portions of the blue-blazed Pocumtuck Ridge Trail in Deerfield, starting from either Pine Nook Road or Keets Road.

DISTANCE 4 Miles   TOWN Colrain
DIFFICULTY RATING Easy/Moderate
TRAIL STYLE Out-and-Back   TRAIL TYPE Doubletrack

The Colrain Ridge Trail runs along a forested north-south ridge between the towns of Colrain and Leyden. Primarily used as a snowmobile and cross-country ski route, the wide old road also makes a fairly nice and relatively easy running route. The trail, which lies entirely on private property but is accessible to the public, used to continue north to the Vermont border but is now closed at the saddle south of Avery Hill. It is blazed with wooden squares, but these are sporadic and unreliable.

DIRECTIONS From exit 26 off I-91 in Greenfield, take Rte. 2 west for 3.5 miles. Turn right on Colrain Shelburne Road, which becomes Greenfield Road, and go north for 4.25 miles. Turn right on West Leyden Road and take an immediate left into a parking area next to Chandler Hill Cemetery. There is space here for several vehicles.

TRAIL From a gate at the parking area, the trail leads north up the hill along the stony access road for several communications towers. It passes right of the towers, leads through another gate, then continues north into the woods up the southwest side of Chandler Hill. After passing through a small clearing, it soon levels off and passes to the right of a large woodland pool, then reaches a 3-way junction on the south side of Taggard Hill at about 0.4 miles. Stay left here. The road climbs up and over the north side of Taggard Hill. The descent on the other side can be somewhat muddy. Continue north at easy grades across an

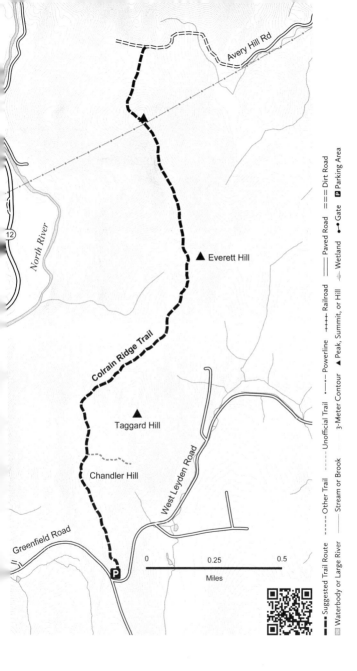

Avery Hill Rd

North River

12

▲ Everett Hill

Colrain Ridge Trail

▲ Taggard Hill

Chandler Hill

West Leyden Road

Greenfield Road

P

0   0.25   0.5

Miles

--- Suggested Trail Route   ----- Other Trail   ------ Unofficial Trail   •—•— Powerline   —— Paved Road   === Dirt Road

Waterbody or Large River   —— Stream or Brook   .... 3-Meter Contour   ▲ Peak, Summit, or Hill   ⊥ Wetland   •—• Gate   P Parking Area undulating series of small hills along the crest of the ridge. At Everett Hill, the road swings slightly left. At about 1.75 miles the roadway becomes grassy as it passes through a small clearing and then climbs up a hill. It emerges at an open powerline swath where there are limited views of the valleys on either side. Continue north down the hill to a partially open field. Stay straight at a junction with a snowmobile trail and reach an east-west oriented old road at a little over 2 miles from the parking area. This is the turnaround point.

NEARBY Just north of Shelburne Falls, a large network of dense, unmarked, and runnable trails threads through Catamount State Forest from Catamount Hill Road and Stacey Road.

Greenfield Ridge

DISTANCE 5 Miles   **TOWN** Greenfield
DIFFICULTY RATING Moderate   **TRAIL STYLE** Loop
TRAIL TYPE Singletrack/Doubletrack

Greenfield Ridge forms a natural wall between the town of Greenfield and the Connecticut River. Neatly bisected by Mountain Road, it consists of Rocky Mountain Park in the north, where the high point is called Poets Seat, and Temple Woods in the south, capped by a rocky ledge called Sachem Head. Both sections are laced with trails. The route described here loops around the entire ridge and passes through a variety of habitats. Though generally of easy to moderate difficulty, some portions are steep and rough, and in some places the route passes near the edge of dangerously steep cliffs.

DIRECTIONS From exit 26 off I-91, take Rte. 2 about 1.25 miles east through the center of Greenfield. Where Rte. 2A turns left, bear right and take Crescent Street 0.45 miles east. Turn right on Parkway South and go 0.3 miles to the large dirt parking area for Temple Woods. A limited amount of parking is also available in the middle of the ridge along Mountain Road.

TRAIL Starting at the parking area, go south on the red-blazed Larry Clark Trail for about 0.3 miles, passing several junctions with a parallel trail on the left. This wide old dirt road, also known as Bears Den Road, is mostly flat with soft footing. Stay straight at a junction where a spur path leads left (east) up a steep set of stairs toward Sachem Head. In about 400 feet, bear right on a green-blazed trail that leads down through a powerline swath and through a cover of forest. Stay straight at an

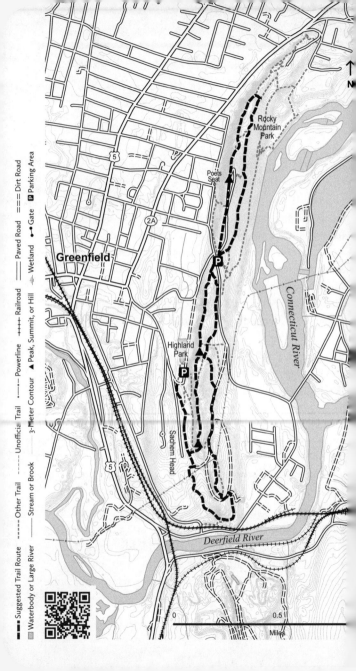

Suggested Trail Route ┃ Other Trail ----- Unofficial Trail ----- Powerline ++++ Railroad ──── Paved Road ═══ Dirt Road

Waterbody or Large River ──── Stream or Brook ─── 3-Meter Contour ▲ Peak, Summit, or Hill ●── Gate 🅿 Parking Area

Greenfield

Rocky Mountain Park

Poets Seat

Highland Park

Sachem Head

Connecticut River

Deerfield River

N ↑

0   0.5
Miles

easily missed junction where the blue-blazed Pocumtuck Ridge Trail descends on the right. Now follow blue and green blazes east back up to a dirt road and a junction labeled Five Points. Go left, following the blue blazes a few hundred feet up to a junction. Take a right and follow the blue-blazed singletrack trail north up and over a low ridge to Bears Den Road. This trail forks almost immediately; the easier right leg rejoins the more rugged left one at the far side of a powerline swath. Stay left where the two legs rejoin and descend to Bears Den Road.

Take a right and follow the dirt road north along the east side of Greenfield Ridge, passing a junction with the blue trail on the left and a wider unmarked junction on the right, for 0.3 miles to a junction. Go left on the orange-blazed singletrack trail and climb gently on soft ground for 0.2 miles to a junction. Go right on the white-blazed trail for 0.1 miles to a 4-way junction. Stay straight, now following red blazes. The trail descends slightly and then climbs to a Y-junction in about 0.4 miles. Follow the blue trail 0.1 miles gently down to the parking area on Mountain Road (be alert crossing the road here). From Mountain Road, go north about 100 feet up the paved road toward Poets Seat, then take a right on the white-blazed trail and follow it north along the east slope of the ridge for 0.8 miles, passing several junctions with yellow-blazed trails on the left.

Alternate Option A red-blazed trail parallels the described route north from Mountain Road and offers a slightly more challenging and longer alternate route. It descends to the right at the edge of the parking area, passes an unmarked junction with a spur path on the left, and then bears left (north) on an old road. It soon passes a utility line and narrows, then runs along the steep hillside for to a junction with the white trail.

At the junction of the white and red trails, go left and quickly reach a junction with the blue trail. Turn left here and follow the blue trail south. It climbs along the crest of the ridge at a gentle grade and reaches the summit of Poets Seat in about 0.3 miles, where there is a fantastic westward view over Greenfield from the top of a steep cliff.

From Poets Seat, descend about 0.4 miles along the paved road back to Mountain Road, carefully cross the road, and follow the blue trail 0.9 miles south along the ridge to Sachem Head. The grade is gentle and the footing occasionally rocky as the trail undulates along minor ups and downs. From the open ledges at the top, take the blue trail steeply down to a junction. Bear right away from the blue trail here and descend a series of steps down to Bears Den Road. Turn right and follow Bears Den Road north back to the parking area.

NEARBY Moderately difficult out-and-back or loop runs can be done along portions of the blue-blazed Pocumtuck Ridge Trail in Deerfield, starting from either Pine Nook Road or Keets Road.

DISTANCE 6.3 Miles **TOWN** Northfield
DIFFICULTY RATING Moderate
TRAIL STYLE Loop **TRAIL TYPE** Doubletrack

Northfield Mountain features a remarkably appealing network of recreational trails on the eastern slopes of the Connecticut River valley. The route described here generally follows the route of a former 10K trail race and primarily utilizes doubletrack trails on old woods roads. As such, it tends to feel more like a cross-country run than a trail run. However, plenty of fun runs of similar distances can be made using combinations of the many narrower, singletrack trails that lace the property within the boundaries of this loop. The Rose Ledge Trail loop is particularly nice for running. Or the two trail types can be combined for a much longer, challenging run utilizing all sorts of terrain.

DIRECTIONS From Rte. 2 at Millers Falls (about 7 miles east of Greenfield), go north on Rte. 63 for 2.25 miles. Turn right onto the entrance road for Northfield Mountain and go 0.15 miles east. Turn right into the visitor center parking lot. From Rte. 10 in the town of Northfield, the site is about 5 miles south on Rte. 63.

TRAIL Starting at the parking area, follow the paved access road north toward a gate. Turn left just before the gate and cross a field on the Tooleybush Turnpike trail (which here is essentially just a mowed path curving to the right across a field), keeping a fenced-in maintenance building on your right. Stay on Tooleybush Turnpike for the rest of the ascent up Northfield Mountain, passing many trail and road intersections along the way, each well marked and numbered with trail signs.

After leaving open fields at about 0.5 miles, the trail enters the woods for a short duration. Then it emerges into a cleared powerline swath at 0.7 miles, which it follows up the hillside, partly on mowed grass and partly on long stretches of wooden planks. Near where the powerlines make a slight turn to the left at around 1.2 miles, the trail veers into the woods on the right. Still gradually ascending, it passes two junctions with Hemlock Trail and one with Ecstasy Ramble Trail, all on the right. Just past this, you encounter the steepest ascent of the run at a pitch called "The Chute," marked by a sign at the top. It's a tough climb, but fairly short. After that, keep climbing at a moderate grade until the road levels out and traverses the slope in a southerly direction.

At about 2.5 miles, the trail crosses the paved access road. Continue running southwest on the wide Tooleybush Turnpike, now undulating some but still gradually ascending. At 3 miles you come to a junction (#32). Turn left here for a short (about 0.25 miles) out-and-back spur trail up to the reservoir at the top. You reach a small loop at the top of the paved road, cross it, and descend slightly to an observation platform near the edge of the water. Once you've taken in the view, return back the way you came.

Back at junction #32, go south on the 10th Mountain Division Trail. Follow this trail for the next 3 miles on your way down the mountain. Most of the descent is gradual, but there are a few quick drops and even a few rises along the way. In about 0.25 miles, pass Hill 'n Dale Trail on the right. Soon after, an unmarked blue-blazed trail leads left; this trail leads about 0.5 miles east and connects with the Metacomet-Monadnock (M-M) Trail above the Briggs Brook cascades.

Continue down the wide and grassy 10th Mountain Division

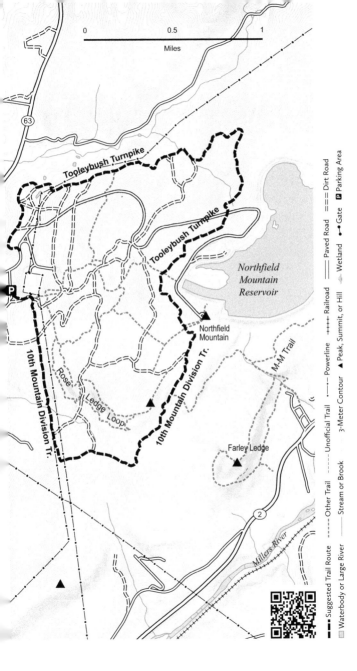

0   0.5   1

Miles

63

Tooleybush Turnpike

Tooleybush Turnpike

Northfield Mountain Reservoir

P

10th Mountain Division Tr.

Rose

Ledge Loop

▲ Northfield Mountain

▲

10th Mountain Division Tr.

M-M Trail

▲ Farley Ledge

2

Millers River

▲

Suggested Trail Route ┊   Other Trail ------   Unofficial Trail ------   Powerline -·-·-·   Railroad ┼┼┼┼   Paved Road ═══   Dirt Road ═══   Gate ●━   **P** Parking Area

Waterbody or Large River ▬▬   Stream or Brook ▬▬   3-Meter Contour ▬▬   ▲ Peak, Summit, or Hill   ⌇ Wetland

Trail, which drops steadily and eventually swings to the right and heads north straight down a powerline corridor. After passing several more trail junctions on the right and one leading to private property on the left, you reach a junction where you make a quick left (west) and then a right to go around a power station. You come out at a field where you bear right to return to the visitor center.

NEARBY An out-and-back run along the M-M Trail from the Farley Ledge area just north of Rte. 2 in Erving climbs for about 2 miles to a beautiful view from ledges overlooking the Millers River gorge.

Mt. Grace

DISTANCE 5.5 Miles **TOWN** Warwick
DIFFICULTY RATING Challenging
TRAIL STYLE Loop **TRAIL TYPE** Singletrack/Doubletrack

At 1,617 ft., Mt. Grace is the third-highest peak in Massachusetts east of the Connecticut River. In a large figure-8 loop, the difficult run described here scales the mountain's north flank, passes by the fire tower at the top, and visits the scenic ledge on Little Mt. Grace. Due to the length and intensity of the ascent, runners will want to be in top shape before attempting this route. Warning: do not attempt to use the 2012 park map for navigation here; it mis-maps some trails on the east side, does not show one trail on the west side, and depicts an inaccurate route for the Metacomet-Monadnock (M-M) Trail on the south side.

DIRECTIONS From Rte. 10/63 in Northfield, go 7.5 miles east up into the hills on Warwick Road, which becomes Northfield Road. In the village of Warwick, turn left onto Rte. 78 and go 0.7 miles to the Mt. Grace State Forest parking area on the left. From Rte. 2A in Orange, go north on Rte. 78 for 6.9 miles to the Mt. Grace State Forest parking area on the left.

TRAIL Starting at the parking area, go north into the open field to a small wooden bridge where the blue-blazed Round the Mountain Trail (RtM Trail) heads into the woods. Continue north on mostly wide singletrack trail, generally descending but with a few climbs now and then. At 1.2 miles, you arrive at a junction with the white-blazed M-M Trail.

Go left at the junction and begin ascending gradually to the

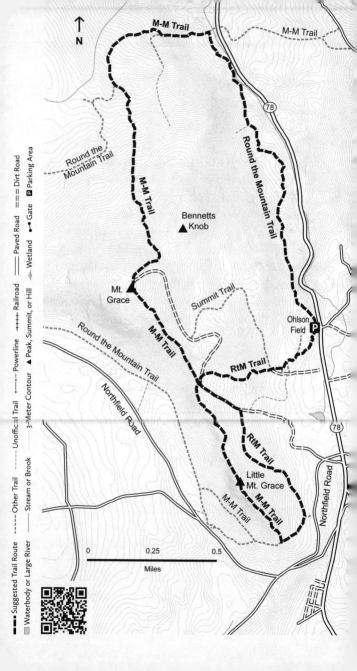

N

M-M Trail

M-M Trail

78

Round the Mountain Trail

Round the Mountain Trail

Bennetts Knob

M-M Trail

Mt. Grace

Summit Trail

Ohlson Field

M-M Trail

RtM Trail

Round the Mountain Trail

Northfield Road

RtM Trail

Little Mt. Grace

M-M Trail

M-M Trail

78

Northfield Road

•••• Suggested Trail Route — — — Other Trail - - - - Unofficial Trail
━ ━ ━ Paved Road ═══ Dirt Road
++++ Railroad •—•—• Powerline ● Gate P Parking Area
━━ 3-Meter Contour ▲ Peak, Summit, or Hill
— Stream or Brook
░ Waterbody or Large River

| 0 | 0.25 | 0.5 |
Miles

west. In 0.25 miles you come to a wooden lean-to shelter. The trail continues up the hill to the left of the shelter. After climbing steadily for 0.3 miles, you reach a junction where the RtM Trail heads off to the right (west) up and then across the slope. This trail looks appealing here, and it may be tempting to consider trying a loop run around the mountain on it. However, at the time of this writing, a recent logging operation has caused the trail to be blocked by slash and downed trees.

From the junction, head up the trail on a sustained, steady climb to the top. The pitch gets steepest just before the top; here the thin nature of mountain soils in New England can be seen along several bedrock exposures where the trail has eroded away. The trail levels off and abruptly runs into a dirt road. It follows the road south across the mostly wooded summit of Mt. Grace to a fire tower in a grassy clearing. The fire tower is usually closed, but there are excellent views in all directions from the top level of the staircase. There are also several picnic tables and a large boulder near the base of the tower.

From the summit, descend to the south on the M-M Trail, initially along the path of a utility line and then through the woods to the side. At a clearing in a flat area about 0.5 miles down from the summit, you reach a junction with the dirt access road. Bear right just before the road and follow the M-M Trail back into the woods.

The next section of trail traverses the narrow ridge of Little Mt. Grace. After rising gradually for 0.5 to the summit, where there is a fine view to the southwest from a ledge, the trail drops steeply for 0.25 miles down to a junction with the RtM Trail.

Turn left here and follow the RtM Trail north along the eastern slope of Little Mt. Grace. In 0.25 miles you pass a short spur path out to Northfield/Wendell Road. Keep heading north and climb steadily for 0.5 miles until you reach a junction with the dirt access road. Turn left and climb steeply up the dirt road for

0.2 miles. About 100 feet past the junction you passed earlier in the grassy clearing at the saddle between the two mountains, bear right on the RtM Trail.

Descend steadily along the RtM Trail until you reach a 4-way intersection where a singletrack trail leads up to the left to the summit and a heavily eroded doubletrack trail leads right. Continue straight here and go 0.25 miles back to the parking area at Ohlson Field, passing several unmarked junctions with trails on the right along the way. Just before coming out into an open field, veer right off the wide trail onto a narrower path that takes you directly back to the parking lot.

NEARBY About 5 miles to the east, the 22-mile Tully Trail loop in Royalston, Warwick, and Orange makes a spectacular and very challenging long run.

DISTANCE 5.5 Miles   **TOWN** Wendell
DIFFICULTY RATING Moderate   **TRAIL STYLE** Loop
TRAIL TYPE Singletrack/Doubletrack/Dirt Road

Located high above the Millers River valley, Wendell State Forest offers a treasure trove of trail running options. Utilizing a variety of trail types, the loop described here visits many of the highlights of the western portion. It also traverses parts of an adjacent conservation property called Hidden Valley Memorial Forest, where there are a number of very nice trails.

DIRECTIONS From Rte. 63 in Millers Falls, take South Prospect Street about 1 mile east. At a fork, stay right and go about 2 miles on Wendell Road. At the Wendell State Forest headquarters building, turn left on Ruggles Pond Road and descend about 0.25 miles to the parking area at the north end of Ruggles Pond. Note the park hours to make sure you don't get locked inside, and park at the headquarters building if you know you will be there after the gate closes.

TRAIL Take the white-blazed Metacomet-Monadnock (M-M) Trail into the woods near some picnic tables at the north end of the parking area. Stay straight at an unmarked junction with a trail on the left, then bear left at a shelter. After crossing a wet spot on wooden bridges and passing through a semi-open dry area, the trail descends at a moderate grade above the east bank of Lyons Brook, where there are several pretty cascades. At 0.6 miles, the trail takes a hard right and climbs briefly along a tributary stream. Then it levels out and enters Hidden Valley Memorial Forest, where it soon reaches a junction with Lynn's Falls Trail.

Optional Trim Bear right on Lynn's Falls Trail and climb steeply for a short distance along a well-constructed section of trail, passing Lynn's Falls and some forested ledges. Go right at a junction with the M-M Trail and then at all remaining junctions to return to the parking area. This short loop is approximately 2.5 miles long.

Go left at the junction with Lynn's Falls Trail. Very soon you reach a junction with an unnamed, blue-blazed trail on the left. Turn left off of the M-M Trail here, cross a stream, and climb through an old timber harvest area. In 0.25 miles, you reach another junction. Go left again and follow the blue-blazed trail up the south side of Jerusalem Hill. After passing a ledge with a nice view to the west, continue north. The trail becomes slightly harder to follow but remains blazed with occasional blue markers. It passes back into Wendell State Forest, crosses over the wooded summit of Jerusalem Hill, then descends the east side of the mountain at a moderate grade over soft pine needles. The next junction is very subtle; be alert and look for a faint trail on the left just before the trail reaches the bottom of the valley.

Optional Trim Stay straight and follow the blue-blazed trail as it swings right and begins climbing at a steady grade. After leveling out, it heads south along the top of a tall cliff hidden in the forest; be mindful of your footing here! At an easily missed fork in the trail, bear left away from the cliffs. At a junction with the M-M Trail, go left and follow it up to Jerusalem Road, then stay right at all remaining junctions.

Heading north from the unmarked junction, follow the sinuous singletrack trail for about 1 mile down to a junction with Davis Road. Go right (east) on the wide road. Pass the lower end of Jerusalem Road on the right, then ascend gently to a 4-way junction. Go right on Damon Camp Road. In 0.1 miles, bear right on the M-M Trail. Take the M-M Trail south up the ridge.

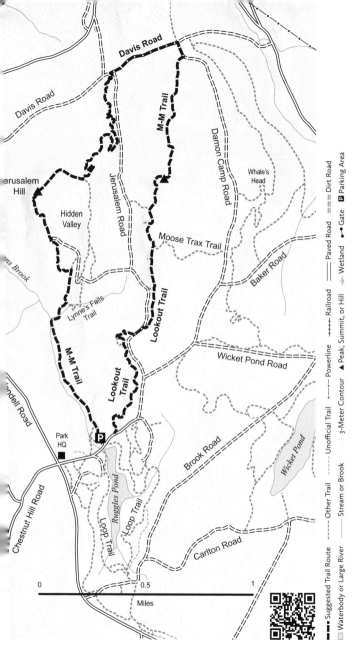

Davis Road

Davis Road

M-M Trail

Jerusalem Hill

Damon Camp Road

Whale's Head

Hidden Valley

Jerusalem Road

Moose Trax Trail

ms Brook

Lynne's Falls Trail

Baker Road

M-M Trail

Lookout Trail

Wicket Pond Road

ndell Road

Lookout Trail

Park HQ

Wicket Pond

Chestnut Hill Road

Brook Road

Loop Trail

Ruggles Pond

Loop Trail

Carlton Road

0   0.5   1

Miles

Suggested Trail Route   ----- Other Trail   ····· Unofficial Trail   •····• Powerline   === Dirt Road

▲ Peak, Summit, or Hill

Waterbody or Large River   Stream or Brook   3-Meter Contour

—— Paved Road   +++ Railroad   ●—● Gate   🅿 Parking Area

〰 Wetland

In 0.8 miles you pass a faint junction with an unmarked side trail on the right that leads down to Jerusalem Road. You then reach the first of two spur trails to nice westward vistas, each marked with "Look Out" signs, on the right. Pass Moose Trax Trail on the left. At a junction where the M-M Trail descends to the right, stay straight.

From the junction with the M-M Trail, follow the blue-blazed Lookout Trail south for 0.2 miles to Jerusalem Road. Turn left and go 300 feet on the road, then bear right off the road at a sign that reads "Trail." In 0.1 miles the trail splits into two roughly equidistant forks for a short distance. The right fork passes an interesting ledge, while the left fork is slightly easier. At 0.7 miles from Jerusalem Road, the trail comes out onto Ruggles Pond Road just up from the pond and parking area.

NEARBY Other worthwhile trail running possibilities can be found at Wendell State Forest, notably in the Wicket Pond and Ruggles Pond vicinities and around Whale's Head and Baker Road. Also, both the Robert Frost Trail and the M-M Trail lead south from Wendell State Forest, offering possible long-distance options through the Pioneer Valley.

33 Mt. Toby

DISTANCE 5 Miles **TOWN** Sunderland
DIFFICULTY RATING Challenging **TRAIL STYLE** Loop
TRAIL TYPE Singletrack/Doubletrack/Dirt Road/Mixed

The broad mass of Mt. Toby and several adjacent summits rise above the Connecticut River in the north-central Pioneer Valley. The dense network of trails in Mt. Toby State Forest allows for a great variety of interesting trail runs of varying difficulty levels. The literal figure-8 loop described here makes use of multiple trail types on the main mountain and a northern spur called Cranberry Ridge.

DIRECTIONS From Rte. 116 in Sunderland, take Rte. 47 north for 4 miles. Turn right on Reservation Road and go east for 0.5 miles to a parking area on the right, where there is space for 7–8 vehicles.

TRAIL From the parking area, follow the trail southwest into the woods behind the trailhead kiosk and stay right at the fork. In about 100 feet, cross the dirt road and take the orange-blazed Robert Frost Trail (RFT) west up the hillside. The trail climbs steeply at first, then bears left and levels off slightly as it traverses the eastern side of Cranberry Ridge. In about 0.5 miles you arrive at a 3-way junction where the RFT bears left. Go straight and climb to the summit of Cranberry Ridge. Bear left at an unmarked junction and begin descending the west slope. Pass an unmarked trail on the right, which leads down to a spur trail to the Sunderland Caves. About 0.25 miles down from the crest of the ridge, take a left on Bridle Path.

Bridle Path leads south along the base of the slope, crosses

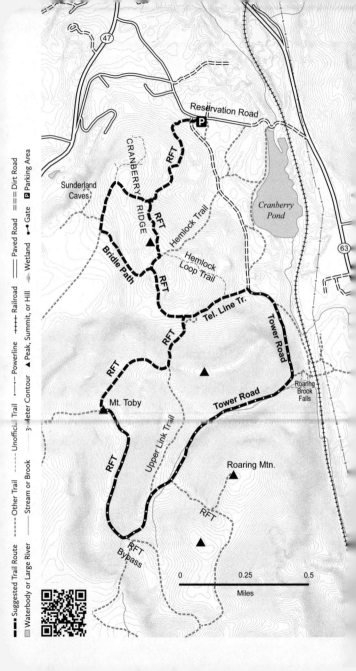

Legend

- ▪▪▪ Suggested Trail Route
- ▬▬ Waterbody or Large River
- ----- Other Trail
- ------ Stream or Brook
- ----- Unofficial Trail
- ------ 3-Meter Contour
- ·-·-· Powerline
- ══ Paved Road
- +++ Railroad
- ══ Dirt Road
- ···· Wetland
- •─ Gate
- P Parking Area

Map Labels

- 47
- Reservation Road
- P
- CRANBERRY RIDGE
- Sunderland Caves
- RFT
- Hemlock Trail
- Cranberry Pond
- Bridle Path
- Hemlock Loop Trail
- 63
- Tel. Line Tr.
- RFT
- Tower Road
- RFT
- Roaring Brook Falls
- Mt. Toby
- Tower Road
- Upper Link Trail
- Roaring Mtn.
- RFT
- RFT
- RFT Bypass

0   0.25   0.5

Miles

a wet area, then slabs diagonally up the hillside at a moderate grade. After making a hard left turn, it climbs gently to a junction with the RFT at the crest of Cranberry Ridge. Turn right on the RFT and climb very briefly, then descend to a junction with the Telephone Line Trail. Bear left and descend the Telephone Line Trail for 0.25 miles to a junction with the dirt access road on the east side of the mountain.

Go right on the access road and follow it south. The road curves around the northeast side of the mountain and soon begins climbing at a steady grade. At a junction on the left, the Roaring Brook Falls Trail leads about 0.1 miles steeply down to Roaring Brook Falls. Continue uphill at a moderate grade along the dirt road alongside Roaring Brook. In about 0.6 miles, pass a junction on the left where the RFT heads steeply southeast up the hill (the spur trail to the summit of Roaring Mountain is rough, poorly marked, and not very good for running). The RFT now coincides with the road all the way to the top. About 0.1 miles up from the RFT junction, pass a junction with the Upper Link Trail on the right.

Optional Trim To avoid going over the summit of Mt. Toby and shorten your run by 0.6 miles, take the mostly flat Upper Link Trail north across the slope to the RFT/Telephone Line Trail.

Keep climbing the access road for another 0.75 miles to the fire tower at the 1,269-ft. summit of Mt. Toby. From the summit, follow the Telephone Line Trail down to the north, occasionally detouring into the woods on the left. This trail is very steep in places and can be slick when wet, especially on the grassier sections. About 0.4 miles from the top, bear left at a marked junction with the Upper Link Trail on the right. About 0.15 miles down another steep section, reach a junction with the RFT. Go left on the RFT and follow it first west then north up and along Cranberry Ridge. Pass junctions with the Bridle Path on the

Climbing the access road at Mt. Toby.

left and the Hemlock Trail on the right. (The Hemlock Trail makes a nice alternate route down; however, the fainter Hemlock Loop Trail is poorly marked and not recommended for running). Keep following the RFT north back down the ridge to the parking area.

NEARBY About 3 miles to the southeast in Leverett, the steep dirt road up through Rattlesnake Gutter makes a great hill workout on town-owned land, and a network of side trails on private land leads east from the northern end of the closed portion of road toward Brushy Mountain.

DISTANCE 4+ Miles **TOWN** South Deerfield
DIFFICULTY RATING Moderate **TRAIL STYLE** Loop
TRAIL TYPE Singletrack/Doubletrack

North Sugarloaf Mountain, along with its lower sister summit, South Sugarloaf, is part of the Mt. Sugarloaf Reservation. It is largely forested and features a network of trails not depicted on most park maps. The route described here utilizes older singletrack hiking trails and doubletrack old roads as well as two newer singletrack trails constructed by mountain bikers. At only 791 feet, the mountain is not particularly high, but getting there makes an excellent hill workout and the descent is fun no matter what route you choose. The trails of North Sugarloaf can be combined with a loop over South Sugarloaf or an out-and-back north on the Pocumtuck Ridge Trail for much longer runs.

DIRECTIONS From exit 24 on I-91, go east on Rte. 116 for 1.4 miles. Then turn left and head north on River Road for 1.5 miles. Turn left on Hillside Avenue. In 0.3 miles, there is a very small parking area on the left with space for about 4 vehicles (make sure to not block the gate).

TRAIL Starting at the parking area, the wide trail heads uphill to the south, first curving right, then left, then running straight—all at a steady, moderate grade. In about 0.5 miles, you reach a 3-way junction. Stay straight and climb straight up the slope at a steeper grade. In 0.3 miles, you reach the crest of the ridge and curve to the right around a swamp to a trail junction. Go left here and head south on an old road toward the summit. It is flat for a short distance, then the grade steepens as it begins to climb via switchbacks. Soon it reaches a junction with a singletrack trail on the left, marked by a stone cairn. Continue south over the wooded summit and descend slightly to a short spur path to a very nice view west from an open ledge.

From the ledge, continue south and begin descending, passing two junctions with a faint bootleg path leading right to a cave on the south face of the hill. Soon, the trail arrives at another junction. Going straight would take you down an extremely steep, eroded trail to the saddle between the two Sugarloaves; go left here. The singletrack trail rises slightly and then traverses a ridge across the upper part of the mountain's south side. Then it descends to a junction with another trail leading right to South Sugarloaf. Go left and descend to an easy-to-miss junction with a trail that runs along an overgrown road leading steeply up to the left. Go right here and descend a short distance to where the trail veers left and crosses the (sometimes dry) brook.

The trail now heads north along the lower slopes of the mountain's east side, climbing some as it does so. Eventually, this trail intersects with the trail you came in on. A few hundred feet before it does, however, take a left at an unmarked junction and make a very runnable loop using two mountain bike trails that climb the slope via twisty, looping switchbacks. In a few hundred feet, you reach a junction where the two trails split. Go left here and climb the slope for about a mile. You will pass two unmarked junctions with spur trails leading off to the left; stay right at both. Near the crest of the ridge, turn right at a junction with the other trail, which descends the slope in much the same manner as the one you just came up. At the bottom, bear left where the two trails converge, then go left at the next junction. Very soon, just after the trail crosses a stream, take a right and follow the wide old road back out to the parking area.

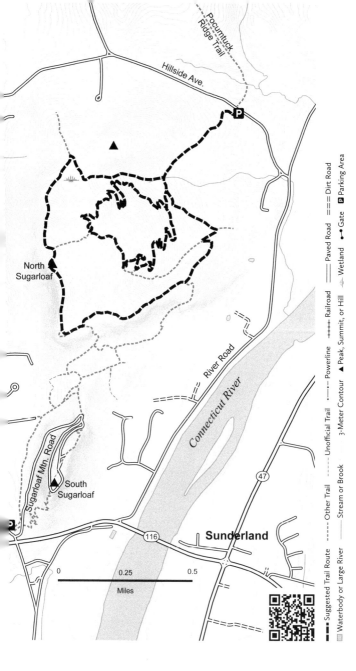

Pocumtuck
Ridge Trail

Hillside Ave.

P

▲

North
Sugarloaf ▲

River Road

Connecticut River

Sugarloaf Mtn. Road

South
Sugarloaf ▲

47

116   **Sunderland**

P

0	0.25	0.5

Miles

▬▬ Suggested Trail Route   ----- Other Trail   ----- Unofficial Trail   ----- 3-Meter Contour   ══ Railroad   ─── Paved Road   ═══ Dirt Road   ●─ Gate   **P** Parking Area

━━━ Waterbody or Large River   ─── Stream or Brook   ••••• Powerline   ~~~ Wetland   ▲ Peak, Summit, or Hill

Optional Extension and/or Starting Point North Sugarloaf Mountain is connected to South Sugarloaf Mountain via a pair of steep, challenging singletrack trails. A longer run incorporating a loop over and around South Sugarloaf can be added to this run, with the added features of a stupendous view from the tower at the summit and nice running over sometimes steep but well-maintained singletrack trails.

NEARBY The Pocumtuck Ridge Trail leads north from the Hillside Road parking area. After a brief descent and two small stream crossings, it climbs to and runs north along the ridge for several miles.

DISTANCE 3.3 Miles   **TOWN** Amherst/Leverett
DIFFICULTY RATING Easy/Moderate
TRAIL STYLE Out-and-Back   **TRAIL TYPE** Singletrack

Puffers Pond in the Factory Hollow/Cushman section of northern Amherst is a very popular swimming spot in summer. It is also the locus of several possible trail run loops that can be cobbled together using the network around the pond, the trails at the Mill River Conservation Area, the Robert Frost Trail on either side of the pond, and the Eastman Brook Conservation Area to the north. The route described here links several of these trails into a series of out-and-backs and loops.

DIRECTIONS From Rte. 9 in Hadley, go north on Rte. 116 for 3.3 miles. Turn right onto Pine Street and go 0.3 miles east to a traffic light. Go left at the light and bear right onto Rte. 63. Go north on Rte. 63 for 0.3 miles. Take a right on Summer Street and go 0.4 miles. Turn left onto Mill Street and immediately turn right for a small parking lot for the Puffers Pond Conservation Area.

From the parking lot, cross a grassy area to a small beach on the west side of the pond, then follow the red-blazed H. H. Jackson Trail (not signed at this end) around the northwest shoreline, just above the waterline. In about 0.25 miles, you reach a junction with the orange-blazed Robert Frost Trail (RFT).

Go north on the RFT and briefly ascend a paved lane beneath a dark conifer canopy. The trail veers left off the lane, climbs a hill, and reaches Pulpit Hill Road. Across the road, follow the RFT past a gate and down a dirt road. The trail soon veers right off the road and becomes singletrack again at an easy-to-miss junction, then climbs to the top of Pulpit Hill. On the other side

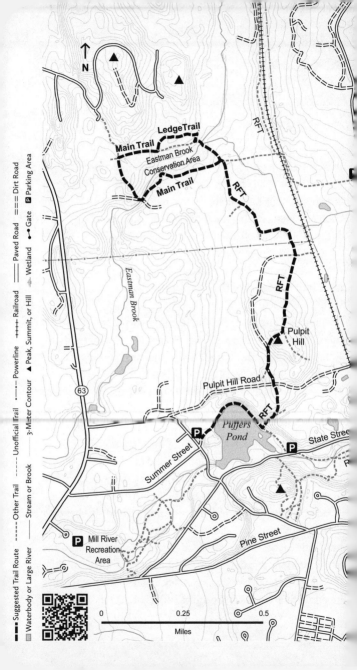

Legend (left margin):

- Suggested Trail Route
- Other Trail
- Unofficial Trail
- Waterbody or Large River
- Stream or Brook
- +++++ Railroad
- -··- Powerline
- === Dirt Road
- Paved Road
- 3-Meter Contour
- ▲ Peak, Summit, or Hill
- ꝫ Wetland
- ◆—○ Gate
- **P** Parking Area

Map labels:

↑ N

Ledge Trail

Main Trail

Eastman Brook Conservation Area

Main Trail

RFT

RFT

Eastman Brook

RFT

▲ Pulpit Hill

Pulpit Hill Road

RFT

P Puffers Pond

P State Street

Summer Street

63

P Mill River Recreation Area

Pine Street

0   0.25   0.5

Miles

of the hill, pass an unmarked junction with a path on the right, and then descend to an unmarked 4-way intersection (left leads to fields and right leads to active railroad tracks). Stay straight on the RFT, gently descending to a powerline crossing. On the other side of the powerline, the trail bears left and crosses a wet area on boardwalks. Then it reaches an unmarked junction and bears right (left leads back out to the powerline) and becomes slightly wider. At another unmarked junction, a trail leads left out to a field. Continue straight on the RFT to a mowed field. Follow the trail along the left (west) side of the field to a junction by a sign for the Eastman Brook Conservation Area, where the RFT turns sharply right. From this junction, the RFT continues east across a somewhat wet area and then turns left along the east edge of a field (where there is a substantial amount of poison ivy).

To run the 0.9-mile loop through the Eastman Brook Conservation Area, follow the red-blazed Ellsworth Barnard Trail. Going counterclockwise, take lefts at all junctions, but make an exception for the yellow-blazed Ledges Trail across a small hill; this trail is slightly longer and a bit more interesting than the somewhat wet section of the main trail that it parallels.

Optional Extension To add a short out-and-back loop through the Lower Mill River Conservation Area downstream from Puffers Pond, go out to Mill Street from the parking area and follow the road south for about 0.1 miles to a bridge over the Mill River. Just past the bridge, bear right into the woods down a set of widely spaced wooden steps. Follow the red-blazed Julius Lester Trail south across the flat riverbank next to the Mill River. In 0.4 miles you arrive at a bridge leading across the river to some recreation fields and an alternate parking area. Just before that bridge, bear left on a yellow-blazed trail called the Jennifer Trail (not named at this junction) and follow it in a partial loop, taking lefts at several junctions and arriving back at the red-blazed trail, taking care to not veer right on any spurs leading out to State Street. Then follow the red-blazed trail back to the parking area.

NEARBY The very runnable Robert Frost Trail heads east from the Puffers Pond area and climbs gradually up and over Mt. Boreas to Atkins Reservoir. From there it climbs more steeply up Poverty Mountain to Mt. Orient (see site 36). About 7 miles up in the hills to the east, a challenging 9-mile loop run is possible on dirt and woods roads in Shutesbury State Forest.

Mt. Orient from Amethyst Brook

DISTANCE 5 Miles **TOWNS** Amherst/Pelham
DIFFICULTY RATING Moderate/Challenging
TRAIL STYLE Out-and-Back/Loop
TRAIL TYPE Singletrack/Doubletrack

Mt. Orient is a prominent ridge rising above the east side of Amherst. This combined out-and-back/loop run from the Amethyst Brook Conservation Area climbs the mountain using mostly singletrack trails and includes a wide variety of terrain types. A highly recommended side trip option to Buffum Falls Conservation Area adds several miles through pleasant hemlock woodlands and passes by numerous brook cascades.

DIRECTIONS From downtown Amherst, take Main Street 1.7 miles east to the parking lot for the Amethyst Brook Conservation Area on the left. There is parking here for about 20 vehicles.

Starting at the parking area, take the wide, mulch-covered trail north out to a field with community gardens, following the orange blazes of the Robert Frost Trail (RFT). At a fork, stay left, then bear slightly right and follow the now-narrower path toward the woods. The trail crosses Amethyst Brook on a wooden bridge, then heads east upstream along the left bank. One small stream channel crossing may be required during high water.

Continue east, passing two wooden bridges on the right as well as several unmarked junctions with intersecting trails leading in either direction, making sure to follow the orange blazes of the RFT. After the trail crosses an old woods road, it swings left near the rusty remains of an old car and begins climbing the slope. The grade is moderate at first but soon levels off. Keep following the orange blazes. The footing is rocky in places. After passing a short braid, it comes out into an open area and reaches an unmarked junction with a trail on the right about 1 mile after the start of the climb.

Stay straight on the RFT and climb more steeply over rugged terrain, past an unmarked junction, for about 0.25 miles to an open ledge on the south ridge of Mt. Orient, where there is an excellent view of the Holyoke Range. From the ledge, keep climbing north on the RFT. The trail undulates along the ridge, gently climbing for about 0.5 miles to an unmarked junction. Turn right on the unblazed trail and descend the east side of the mountain. At first the trail leads north, then it curves right and descends south at a moderate grade over very runnable terrain. About 0.6 miles from the junction, turn right at the powerline and go 0.25 miles south at an easy grade to a junction with a dirt road where the lines bend left.

Optional Extension To run the Buffum Brook loop, descend steeply alongside the powerline to Buffum Road. Go left on the paved road for about 0.1 miles to a small sign on the right side of the road. Descend the path to a junction on the other side of a wide wooden bridge. From here, several route options are possible. A loop around the blue-blazed outer perimeter is about 1.5 miles and passes through pleasant hemlock woods over gentle terrain, with several scenic cascades in the rocky stream ravines. The total side trip will add a little over 2 miles to your run.

Turn right on the road and go 0.3 miles northwest over rolling ground back to a junction with the RFT, passing several unmarked junctions along the way. Here, turn left and go back down the way you came on the RFT. Back at Amethyst Brook, take a left at the first wooden bridge to return a slightly different

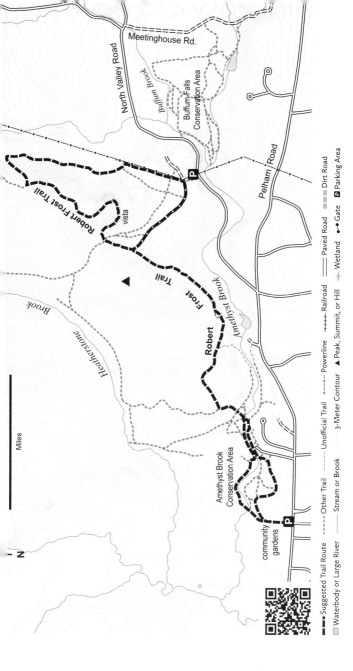

Miles

N

Meetinghouse Rd.

North Valley Road

Buffum Brook

Buffum Falls Conservation Area

Pelham Road

Robert Frost Trail

vista

Heatherstone Brook

Robert Frost Trail

Amethyst Brook

Amethyst Brook Conservation Area

community gardens

Legend

- Suggested Trail Route
- Waterbody or Large River
- Other Trail
- Stream or Brook
- Unofficial Trail
- ····· 3-Meter Contour
- —— Paved Road
- ···· Powerline
- Wetland
- === Dirt Road
- +++ Railroad
- ▲ Peak, Summit, or Hill
- •→ Gate
- P Parking Area

way. Take a right on the other side of the bridge and follow any of the yellow-blazed trails west along the south side of the brook to arrive back at the community gardens where you started.

NEARBY The Metacomet-Monadnock (M-M) Trail passes over Mt. Lincoln and through a network of woods roads in Cadwell Memorial Forest in Pelham; various loop options are possible from a parking area along Enfield Road and the newly rerouted section of the M-M Trail leading north to the Amherst-Pelham Road features several miles of very nice running.

DISTANCE 5 Miles   **TOWN** Northampton
DIFFICULTY RATING Easy/Moderate   **TRAIL STYLE** Figure-8 Loop
TRAIL TYPE Mostly Singletrack, with some Doubletrack and Dirt Road

Dense with multiple trail types, the Fitzgerald Lake Conservation Area offers an appealing number of possible route configurations. The figure-8 loop described here starts at the parking area on North Farm Road, but good options are also possible starting from Cooke Avenue and Marian Street. There are no big hills or stream crossings, but the terrain is mostly rolling and the singletrack paths can be rocky, rooty, and wet in places.

DIRECTIONS From Rte. 5/10 (King Street) in Northampton, take Bridge Street west for 1.7 miles. Turn right on Mountain Street and go 0.3 miles northwest. Merge right onto North Farm Road and go 0.3 miles north to a parking area on the right, where there is space for 6–8 vehicles.

TRAIL Starting at the parking area, follow the paved access trail northeast into the woods, passing numbered posts next to several natural features. In 0.2 miles, the pavement stops at a junction by a wooden bridge over a wet area. To the right, a long wooden boardwalk leads a few hundred feet out to a dock in the marsh. Cross the zigzag bridge and go right at a trail junction on the wide, white-blazed Fishing Place Trail. Follow this trail beneath dark conifers for 0.2 miles out to a point at the edge of the lake. Pass a beaver lodge and turn left, crossing over wet areas on boardwalks, and go west to a junction with the blue-blazed Lake Trail.

At the junction, turn right and cross the stream. Immediately

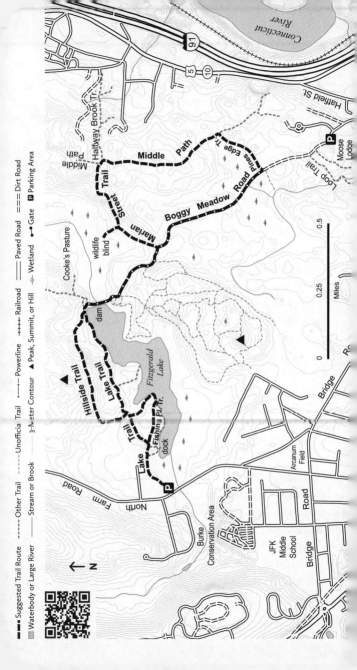

after the stream, turn left at the next junction onto the red-blazed Hillside Trail. This singletrack trail starts out flat and crosses a wet area on wooden planks. Then it climbs partway up the hill and becomes drier. It soon swings right and traverses the slope. Then it drops gradually over rocky ground, and, about 0.5 miles from where it began, arrives at another junction with the Lake Trail. Go straight (east) here. Pass a junction (where the Lake Trail leads left toward Cooke's Pasture) and cross an open area that is often a bit wet before heading out onto the top of the dam at the northern edge of the lake.

At the southern end of the dam, go southeast on a wide old woods road called Boggy Meadow Road. Curving around a rise and passing several unmarked junctions on the right, follow the road south for about 0.25 miles to a junction with the Marian Street Trail on the left.

Continue south on Boggy Meadow Road. In 0.25 miles you arrive at a junction with the Pines Edge Trail on the left.

Optional Extension Continue south for another 0.25 miles on Boggy Meadow Road to an unmarked junction on the right with the Loop Trail. This half-mile long singletrack trail makes a very nice, undulating circuit through the woods, crossing a stream on bridges and reconnecting with Boggy Meadow Road very close to where it started. When done, return back to the unmarked junction.

Go left (north) on the Pines Edge Trail. It crosses a wet area on the right side of a forested swamp, then rises to a junction with the Middle Path on an upland ridge. Go left (north) at the junction and follow the very runnable Middle Path for about 0.5 miles to a 4-way intersection with the blue-blazed Marian Street Trail. Go left on the Marian Street Trail and descend about 0.25 miles to a short spur path on the right that leads to a wildlife blind next to a scenic marsh. In another 0.2 miles, the trail reconnects with Boggy Meadow Road.

Go right and follow Boggy Meadow Road back to the dam. Re-cross the dam and return to the junction of the Lake Trail and Hillside Trail north of the lake. Go left and follow the blue-blazed Lake Trail west for about a mile back to the parking area.

Optional Extension About 0.2 miles along the Lake Trail, the Narrows Trail leads left to a point along the lake. This worthwhile out-and-back extension will add about 0.5 miles.

Alternate Options The unmarked junctions along Boggy Meadow Road all lead to an incredibly dense, unmarked network of trails. A particularly scenic singletrack trail loops down around a peninsula along the east shore of the lake near the dam. These trails are all fun to explore and run on, but many junctions look similar and it is very easy to get disoriented, so allow plenty of time for navigating if you choose to venture out on them.

NEARBY Local runners compete in weekly cross-country races on trails next to the Northampton Community Gardens, about 3 miles to the south.

DISTANCE 4 Miles   **TOWN** Northampton
DIFFICULTY RATING Moderate   **TRAIL STYLE** Lollipop Loop
TRAIL TYPE Singletrack/Doubletrack

Not far from downtown Northampton, the Mineral Hills Conservation Area offers a relatively crowd-free trail running experience in a beautiful wooded setting. The trails are well marked, with helpful numbered signs at all junctions. The complex lollipop-style loop run described here utilizes many of the property's trails, though other combinations are certainly possible. There are significant hills to climb and the trail can be rocky in a few places, but in general this is a fairly gentle run.

DIRECTIONS From Northampton, take Rte. 66 west for about 5 miles. Turn right on West Farms Road and go north for 0.7 miles. At a 4-way intersection, continue straight on Sylvester Road. Go north for 0.2 miles to the Mineral Hills Conservation Area parking lot on the left. There is space here for 4 vehicles. You can also park by the gate at the upper end of Turkey Hill Road.

TRAIL At the parking area along Sylvester Road, the trail starts behind an informational kiosk sign with a map of the property. It heads north and then west across a somewhat wet area, at first keeping an open field on the right. Then, using dock-like aluminum walkways, it crosses several small streams in a scenic wetland. Look for a profusion of yellow marsh marigold flowers blooming here in early spring, and other flowers such as irises and violets a few weeks later. After the wetland, the trail climbs over rocky and rooty terrain to a junction (#101) about 0.25 miles from the parking area.

Take a right on the wide Nedobak Trail and proceed slightly

downhill, crossing several wet areas on boardwalks. In about 0.25 miles, turn left onto Oogamak Trail at junction #102 (a former trail leading off to the right is blocked off, so this location isn't really a junction as much as it is a direction shift and trail name change). From here, climb at a moderate grade for about 500 feet to a junction (#103) with Freda's Trail. Continue straight and keep climbing gradually for about 0.5 miles to junction #104. Turn right onto Ravine Trail. This trail traverses the slope at first, then dips into a ravine, crosses a stream, and begins climbing the slope on the other side. In about 0.5 miles, it arrives at junction #105. Bear right here and begin ascending the Summit Trail. In a little over 0.25 miles, the trail reaches the top of the westernmost summit of Mineral Hills, where there is a bench and a limited view to the west.

From the top, descend south on Summit Trail. Following several switchbacks across the slope, the trail drops steadily for about 0.5 miles to a 4-way intersection (#115) along a wide dirt road. Turn left on Stagecoach Trail and follow it east to an unmarked junction. Here, you have the option of either continuing straight to one of the next numbered junctions (#112 or #111) and then turning left, or taking an immediate left on a short, rough path toward the abandoned quarry. Since it's worth a look, take a left and circle the quarry clockwise on the Quarry Loop Trail. Be careful if you approach the edge of the quarry; it is not blocked off and there's quite a drop. In about 0.25 miles, you arrive at junction #113 on the opposite side. Turn left here and descend into the woods on a short connector trail to junction #106. Take a right and follow another short connector trail to junction #107. Turn left onto Kohl Trail and follow it along mostly flat terrain for about 0.25 miles to junction #108. Continue straight on Kohl Trail to a junction (#109) with Nedobak Trail. Take Nedobak Trail back to junction #101, where you turn right and follow the trail out the way you came in.

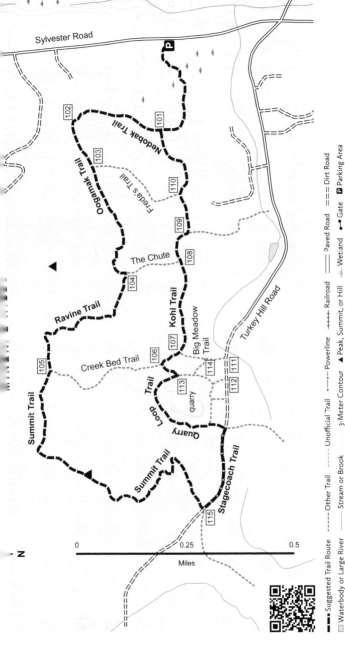

Sylvester Road

P

102

101

Nedobak Trail

103

Oogamak Trail

Freda's Trail

110

109

The Chute

108

104

Ravine Trail

Kohl Trail

Big Meadow Trail

105

107

106

Creek Bed Trail

114

111

113

112

quarry

Quarry Loop Trail

Summit Trail

Summit Trail

Stagecoach Trail

115

Turkey Hill Road

N

0   0.25   0.5

Miles

Suggested Trail Route   ----- Other Trail   ----- Unofficial Trail   ----- Powerline   ++++ Railroad   === Dirt Road

Waterbody or Large River   —— Stream or Brook   ≈ Wetland   ▲ Peak, Summit, or Hill   —— Paved Road   • Gate   P Parking Area

3-Meter Contour

Optional Extension From junction #108, you can lengthen the run slightly by taking an alternate route back to the parking lot. At junction #108, turn left and climb the steep Chute Trail partway up the slope to junction #104. Turn right and follow a 0.25-mile section of Oogamak Trail; this is a gentle, fun descent. At junction #103, take a right and follow Freda's Trail south across mostly level ground. It passes over a wet area on board bridges, and in about 1,000 feet arrives at junction #110. Turn left here and descend gradually on Nedobak Trail to junction #101. From here, turn right and follow the trail back out to the parking area.

NEARBY An extensive network of unmarked trails winds through Sawmill Hills Conservation Area about 2 miles to the northeast.

DISTANCE 8 Miles **TOWNS** Holyoke/Easthampton
DIFFICULTY RATING Challenging
TRAIL STYLE Out-and-Back/Loop **TRAIL TYPE** Singletrack

One of the most iconic landscape features in western Massachusetts, Mt. Tom is laced with a fantastic network of trails and offers many opportunities for exciting running adventures. The route described here climbs the east side of the mountain, does an out-and-back to the summit along the upper rim of spectacularly scenic, precipitous western cliffs, and crosses the crest of the ridge through the interior section of the property before descending back to Lake Bray. *Extreme caution is advised to runners along the cliffs!* In general, the trails are all well marked, easy to follow, and a lot of fun to run.

DIRECTIONS From exit 17 off I-91 in Holyoke, go north on Rte. 5 for about 4 miles to Reservation Road on the left, or, from exit 18 off I-91 in Northampton, go south on Rte. 5 for about 3 miles to Reservation Road on the right. Go west on Reservation Road, pass the fee station at the entrance to Mt. Tom State Reservation, and park in the lot just past the restrooms at the northwest corner of Lake Bray. Note that vehicles must be outside the gate by the posted time, which at some times of the year is as early as 4 p.m.; limited parking is available outside the gate on Reservation Road.

TRAIL Starting at the parking area, go south for 0.1 miles on the wide universal access trail. Take a right at the start of Kay Bee Trail and climb steeply, sometimes via looping switchbacks, for about 0.3 miles. Cross over the Link Trail and continue climb-

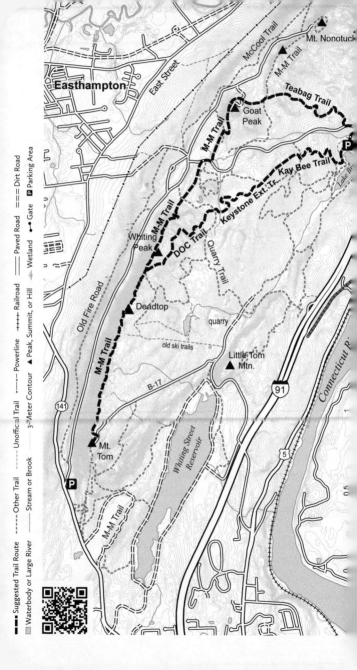

Mt. Nonotuck

McCool Trail

M-M Trail

Teabag Trail

East Street

Easthampton

Goat Peak

M-M Trail

P

Kay Bee Trail

Keystone Ext. Tr.

Lake Bri

M-M Trail

DOC Trail

Whiting Peak

Quarry Trail

Old Fire Road

Deadtop

quarry

old ski trails

Little Tom Mtn.

91

Connecticut R.

B-17

141

5

Mt. Tom

Whiting Street Reservoir

P

M-M Trail

0.5

1

Suggested Trail Route
Waterbody or Large River
Other Trail
Unofficial Trail
Stream or Brook
Powerline
Railroad
3-Meter Contour
Paved Road
Dirt Road
Wetland
Peak, Summit, or Hill
Gate
Parking Area

ing, now at a more moderate grade, for another 0.3 miles. At a 4-way intersection, stay straight and follow Keystone Extension Trail over undulating, ledgy terrain for about 0.6 miles to a 4-way intersection just past a small bridge. Cross over Quarry Trail and ascend DOC Trail for 0.8 miles. The trail rises in a step-like fashion over a series of exposed bedrock ledges, with occasional steeper pitches interspersed with relief-giving flatter sections. At the crest of the ridge, it reaches a junction with the Metacomet-Monadnock (M-M) Trail.

> *Optional Trim* From here, it is possible to skip the out-and-back along the cliffs to the summit and return via the M-M and Teabag Trails for a loop of about 5 miles.

Head south on the M-M Trail for a 2.5-mile round-trip out-and-back run to the summit. WARNING: This section traverses the upper edge of steep west-facing cliffs. It is one of the most dangerous trails in this guide, and runners in particular must be extremely mindful of their footing. That said, it is very popular with trail runners, and with good reason: the scenery is truly top-notch and the sense of adventure palpable. The trail first rises at a moderate grade and crosses over a section of ridge called Deadtop, then descends to the first of several saddles. From here, it rises and falls many times along the way to the summit, often over steep traprock ledges that require some scrambling and use of your hands. At the 1,202-ft. summit, enjoy the southwest view next to the antenna farm, which is also the site of a former summit hotel, then return back the way you came.

From the junction with DOC Trail, head north on the M-M Trail and climb up and over Whiting Peak, where there are more excellent views from open ledges. The descent from Whiting is very steep in places, at one point dropping down a rocky chute that requires the use of your hands. In about 0.5 miles, cross over Quarry Trail and continue north at a gentle grade to the

Cascade Brook at Mt. Tom.

paved auto road. Go right on the road for a few hundred feet, then continue north on the M-M Trail where it re-enters the woods. In about 0.3 miles, the trail swings hard right at a junction with Dynamite Trail and begins a steep climb of Goat Peak. From the top of Goat Peak, descend east for about 0.25 miles, crossing an access road along the way. Pass the upper end of Beau Bridge Trail, and reach the upper end of Teabag Trail a few feet later. Turn right and descend the fun, roller coaster-like Teabag Trail for about 0.8 miles to the auto road. Then follow the auto road back to the parking area.

NEARBY Several of the trails on the north and west sides of Mt. Tom are also excellent for running, including the Old Fire Road Trail, the John McCool Trail, and the Keystone Trail. It is also possible to descend the *very* steep M-M Trail down the south side of Mt. Tom and return to the Lake Bray area via any number of trails heading north from the Whiting Reservoir area.

Lake Bray

DISTANCE 3.5–5 Miles   **TOWN** Holyoke
DIFFICULTY RATING Moderate   **TRAIL STYLE** Loop
TRAIL TYPE Singletrack/Doubletrack

Situated in a valley well below the summit ridge of Mt. Tom, the scenic Lake Bray is separated from the Connecticut River by a low, secondary ridge to the east. This run crosses land owned by the Massachusetts Department of Conservation and Recreation (DCR) and The Trustees of Reservations (TTOR). It follows a loop encircling the pond and the stream that drains into it, with an out-and-back spur to Little Tom Mountain, the highest point along the secondary ridge. There are two options for shortening the route and many options for lengthening it. In general, the extensive trail network at the Mt. Tom State Reservation offers a tremendous wealth of running possibilities, with countless possible variations on distance and difficulty.

DIRECTIONS From exit 17 off I-91 in Holyoke, go north on Rte. 5 for about 4 miles to Reservation Road on the left, or, from exit 18 off I-91 in Northampton, go south on Rte. 5 for about 3 miles to Reservation Road on the right. Go west on Reservation Road, pass the fee station at the entrance to Mt. Tom State Reservation, and park in the lot just past the restrooms at the northwest corner of Lake Bray. Note that vehicles must be outside the gate by the posted time, which at some times of the year is around 4 pm. Limited parking is available outside the gate on Reservation Road.

TRAIL Starting at the parking area, run east back along the access road to the trailhead at the northeastern shore of Lake

Bray. Go south on the blue-blazed Bray Loop Trail. Soon, the trail splits, with a high water option on the left and a potentially muddy option along the water's edge on the right. The two paths converge soon after. In 0.2 miles, you arrive at a junction by a wooden bridge where the Bray Inner Loop Trail leads back to the parking area along the western side of the pond. Continue following the Bray Loop Trail south. Soon, it begins to climb the slope of the ridge on the left. At 0.3 miles from the previous junction, you arrive at 3-way junction.

Optional Trim The Bray Loop Trail goes right here and can be followed back to the parking area for a fairly easy run of about 2.5 miles.

Go left on Knox Trail and immediately ascend the slope at a very steep grade. It soon levels off and follows the crest of the ridge south through the forest, eventually descending to a junction with a wider trail along an old road. Going left leads to a partial view to the east next to a billboard sign in a grassy clearing. Take a right and follow the old road. In a few hundred feet, you arrive at a sign marking the start of TTOR's Woodland Trail to Little Tom Mountain.

You could shorten this run by continuing straight on Knox Trail, but go left and take the Woodland Trail south for a very nice out-and-back lollipop. It climbs for just over 0.5 miles, occasionally via small switchbacks, to a short loop trail just below the top of the hill. Topping out at around 600 feet, the trail does not go all the way to the top, but you could bag the summit with a short bushwhack and a short spur path that leads west to a small woodland pond. To return, run back along the Woodland Trail to Knox Trail.

From the junction with the Woodland Trail, continue west on Knox Trail, which soon swings south and drops slightly to cross Bray Brook before turning and climbing very steeply due

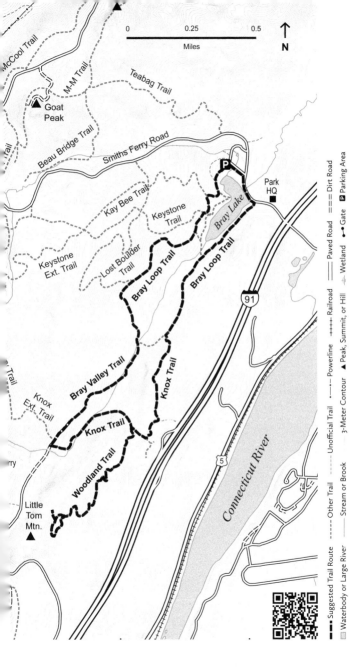

McCool Trail

M-M Trail

▲ Goat Peak

Beau Bridge Trail

Teabag Trail

Smiths Ferry Road

Kay Bee Trail

Keystone Trail

Keystone Ext. Trail

Lost Boulder Trail

Bray Loop Trail

Bray Loop Trail

Bray Lake

Park HQ

I-91

Bray Valley Trail

Knox Trail

Knox Ext. Trail

Knox Trail

Woodland Trail

▲ Little Tom Mtn.

Connecticut River

0   0.25   0.5

Miles

N

Suggested Trail Route ----- Other Trail ----- Unofficial Trail === Dirt Road — Paved Road +++ Railroad ···· Powerline ╫ Wetland 🅿 Parking Area •— Gate — Stream or Brook ▲ Peak, Summit, or Hill ‑‑‑ 3-Meter Contour

Waterbody or Large River

west up to a meadow just north of an old quarry. At a 3-way junction, Knox Trail ends. Turn right and go north here on the Bray Valley Trail, passing a junction with the lower end of Knox Extension Trail on the left and descending gradually through another meadow. The trail then enters the woods and drops steeply down to the brook, which it crosses several times in an area that is frequently wet and muddy.

At a 3-way junction, cross the stream on a small bridge and go north on the Bray Loop Trail. The trail climbs up the slope at first, then levels off and descends at a moderate grade. Pass a junction with the white-blazed Lost Boulder Trail on your left, which you could take to lengthen your run by another mile or so. Continuing straight (north), the Bray Loop Trail keeps traversing the slope and finally drops down to a 3-way junction. Go left here and follow the wide gravel path, called the Lake Bray Universal Access Trail, back to the parking lot. There are numerous junctions in quick succession in this area, but just keep heading north, keeping the pond on your right, to arrive at the parking area.

NEARBY About 2 miles to the southwest in Holyoke, you can run an easy 3.5-mile loop around Whiting Street Reservoir, all on mostly level dirt roads.

DISTANCE 4.5 Miles   **TOWNS** Hadley/South Hadley
DIFFICULTY RATING Moderate/Challenging
TRAIL STYLE Loop   **TRAIL TYPE** Singletrack/Doubletrack

Rising abruptly from the fertile lowlands flanking the Connecticut River, the rolling profile of the Holyoke Range stands out dramatically and features remarkably diverse terrain types, from soft forest floors to rugged, rocky ridges. Unique among New England mountains for its east-west orientation, the Range supports one of the largest and most complex trail networks in the region and is very popular with trail runners. The route described here explores both north and south sides of the ridge and lies almost entirely within Skinner State Park.

DIRECTIONS From exit 19 on I-91, go 0.5 miles east on Rte. 9. Turn right on Bay Road and go east 1.2 miles to where it joins Rte. 47. Then go south on Rte. 47 for 2.3 miles to the trailhead on the left side of the road, where there is space for about 30 vehicles.

TRAIL From the trailhead, go past the gate and follow the wide path a few hundred feet up to an unmarked junction. Bear left at this junction and go another few hundred feet up to marker #139. From here, the yellow-blazed Taylor Notch Trail bears left and briefly heads east across the slope. This trail is in excellent condition and makes for a very pleasant and attractive ascent to the ridge. It soon swings right and begins climbing moderately to the south. The grade steepens as the trail approaches Taylor Notch, rising out of a drainage ravine and up onto a drier slope. Then it briefly levels out again before making a final steep climb to Mountain Road.

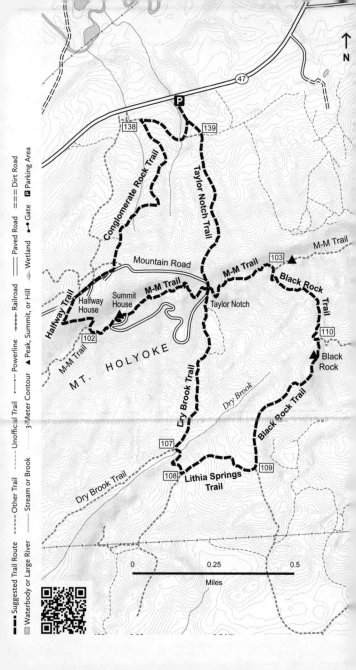

From the trail sign in the notch, go left on the white-blazed Metacomet-Monadnock (M-M) Trail. The grade is gradual at first as the trail angles to the right up a well-constructed side-hill traverse, then gets steeper as it climbs over a series of ledges. About 300 yards from the notch, the trail swings past an open ledge with one of the finest views in the range. From there, climb east up and over the first of a series of small peaks between Mt. Hitchcock and Mt. Holyoke called the Seven Sisters. About 0.3 miles east of Taylor Notch, reach a junction at marker #103. Take a right and descend along the blue-blazed Black Rock Trail. One of the more remote trails in the range, it is fairly steep but in good shape. It reaches a small saddle where there is a junction at marker #110. Turn right and climb for 0.1 miles to the wooded summit of Black Rock, where there is a semi-cleared view of Lithia Springs Reservoir. From here, head southwest down the slope at a gentle grade for 0.4 miles and reach a 3-way junction at marker #109.

Turn right on the yellow-blazed Lithia Springs Trail and descend gradually to a 3-way junction at marker #108. Go right and switchback west down a slope for 0.1 miles to a junction at marker #107. Go right and ascend steadily on the red-blazed Dry Brook Trail for 0.5 miles back to the junction with the M-M Trail at the road in Taylor Notch. Take a left on the M-M Trail and ascend somewhat steeply up the eastern slope of Mt. Holyoke. The trail emerges from the woods at a clearing and follows occasional white blazes west across the open picnic area, then arrives at the Summit House on top of 940-ft. Mt. Holyoke.

From the summit, descend the M-M Trail to a saddle and a junction at marker #102. Go straight on the blue-blazed Halfway Trail, which descends 0.2 miles to the auto road in one big switchback. The grade is moderate at first, then becomes steeper when the trail makes a hairpin turn to the right about halfway down. Take care running down this trail, particularly at the sharp turn, where many loose rock shards cover the ground. At the road, turn right and go 0.2 miles east, past the Halfway House, up to a gate on the left.

Descend at an easy grade on the red-blazed Conglomerate Rock Trail, which is in good condition and fun to run down. Just below the auto road, go straight at a four-way junction with a snowmobile trail, then continue descending. Just below an easily missed trail leading off to the left, pass the 10-foot high boulder called Conglomerate Rock, then descend at a moderate grade for 0.4 miles to an unmarked junction (marker #138 is at a different junction a few hundred feet to the west). Take a right and go about 0.1 miles, ascending slightly, then cross a small wooden bridge and immediately take a left at an unmarked junction. Go a few hundred feet to another unmarked junction, turn left again, and follow the wide path downhill back to the trailhead.

NEARBY Just to the southeast, several good loop runs can be made using marked and unmarked trails in the Lithia Springs Reservoir area.

DISTANCE 6.5 Miles   **TOWNS** Hadley
DIFFICULTY RATING Moderate/Challenging (due to navigation)
TRAIL STYLE Loop   **TRAIL TYPE** Singletrack

Quietly nestled into northern slope of the Holyoke Range lies an amazingly intricate network of mostly unmarked trails known as Earls Trails. Although several of the trails are older dirt roads and hiking trails that show up on park maps, the majority are newer singletrack routes built and maintained by the local mountain biking community. Compared to the Bachelor Street network (see chapter 44), these trails are easier and less technical overall, but navigation is a significant challenge. Due to the extreme density and complexity of the trails, a detailed route is not listed for this site. Rather, a suggested route is provided on the map and the general vicinity described. Runners are encouraged to explore and get to know the site over the course of multiple visits. While it is certainly confusing, it's also very fun, and you can go for hours, racking up many miles without ever repeating a single section of trail.

DIRECTIONS From exit 19 on I-91, go 0.5 miles east on Rte. 9. Turn right on Bay Road and go east 1.2 miles to where it joins Rte. 47. Then go south on Rte. 47 for 1.7 miles. Turn left on Chmura Road and follow it 1.3 miles to a bulb at the end where there is parking for 25–30 vehicles. Do not park in front of the dirt road or block the private driveway. Alternate parking and another entrance to this trail network is located at a dirt road along the east edge of a field just west of the Hadley–Amherst town line, and about 0.5 miles west of Atkins Farms. Should you choose to park here, make sure to pull off to the east side of the

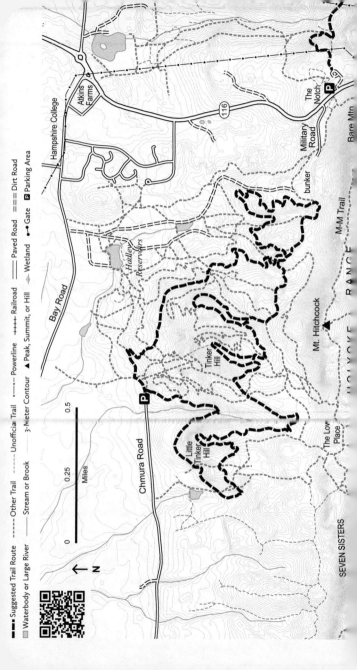

Map Legend

- ∎ ∎ Suggested Trail Route
- - - - Other Trail
- ----- Unofficial Trail
- ·-·-· Powerline
- +++ Railroad
- ==== Paved Road
- === Dirt Road
- —— 3-meter Contour
- —— Stream or Brook
- ▲ Peak, Summit, or Hill
- ⬛ Waterbody or Large River
- ◆ Wetland
- •— Gate
- 🅿 Parking Area

N ←

Miles
0   0.25   0.5

Hampshire College

Atkins Farms

Bay Road

116

Military Road

The Notch

🅿

Bare Mtn

bunker

Hadley Reservoirs

Chmura Road

🅿

Tinker Hill

Little Tinker Hill

Mt. Hitchcock

The Lo_ Place

M-M Trail

HOLYOKE RANGE

SEVEN SISTERS

dirt road, and do not block the gate. A third approach to the site is via Military Road off of Rte. 116, with parking at The Notch.

TRAIL Starting at the Chmura Road parking area, find the start of the red-blazed College Trail by first going east about 100 feet to a junction marked #143 at the base of an old ski lift path. (It is also marked with a small wooden sign on a tree.) Head southwest up the slope of Tinker Hill, climbing at a steady grade. In about 800 feet, take a right at a 4-way intersection where a singletrack trail crosses the wide lane. From here, follow the singletrack trail to the east around the north side of Little Tinker Hill. Staying straight at all junctions for at least the next 2 miles, you gradually climb up and over Little Tinker Hill. It is possible to shorten the run at any time, but the suggested route then goes over Tinker Hill, meanders around on its eastern slope, and traverses the north slope of the Holyoke Range almost as far east as Military Road. Then it descends slightly and crosses the slope in the other direction, with many curves, swoops, and switchbacks along the way, eventually arriving back at the base of the old ski lift.

NEARBY Just uphill from this site, the popular and extremely challenging 12-mile Seven Sisters Trail Race takes place each year in early May, running from The Notch to Rte. 47 and back along the crest of the Holyoke Range on the Metacomet-Monadnock (M-M) Trail.

Holyoke Range
MT. NORWOTTUCK

DISTANCE 6 Miles **TOWN** Amherst
DIFFICULTY RATING Moderate/Challenging
TRAIL STYLE Lollipop Loop **TRAIL TYPE** Singletrack/Doubletrack

Managed by the Massachusetts Department of Conservation and Recreation (DCR), Mt. Holyoke Range State Park covers a large portion of the eastern half of the Holyoke Range. Undoubtedly the most popular attraction is 1,106-ft. Mt. Norwottuck, the highest peak in the range. The route described here includes the summit as well as the Horse Caves, Rattlesnake Knob, and portions of the Metacomet-Monadnock (M-M) Trail and the Robert Frost Trail (RFT).

DIRECTIONS From either the north or the south, take Rte. 116 to The Notch at the top of the pass in the middle of the Holyoke Range, just north of the quarry. Turn east into the visitor center parking lot. There is space here for about 50 cars. This trailhead can be very crowded any time of the year, but especially on weekends and holidays.

TRAIL Starting at the trailhead in The Notch, follow the visitor center driveway on the right up to a wooden sign. From the sign, take the white-blazed M-M Trail, which is concurrent with the orange-blazed RFT for the next 0.5 miles, east into the woods and quickly arrive at an unmarked junction. Veer left on a recent re-routing of the main trail and follow combined white, orange, and blue blazes out to the powerline swath, where the trail turns left. Follow the middle of the powerline corridor for about 100 feet. At the next utility pole, bear right. The trail soon drops steeply down to the Trolley Bed Trail. Turn right and go a few

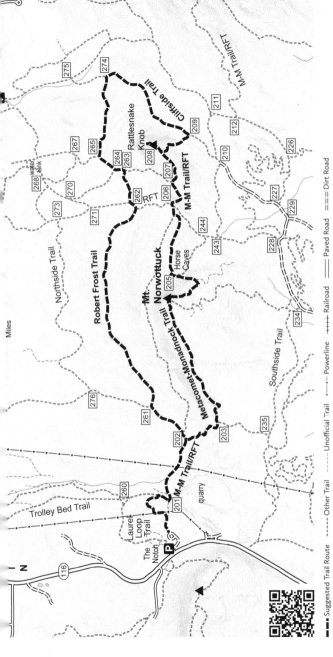

Miles

N

116

The Notch

P

Trolley Bed Trail

Laurel Loop Trail

quarry

M-M Trail/RFT

Northside Trail

Robert Frost Trail

water tank

RFT

Rattlesnake Knob

Cliffside Trail

M-M Trail/RFT

Mt. Norwottuck

Metacomet-Monadnock Trail

Horse Caves

Southside Trail

M-M Trail/RFT

201
202
203
205
206
207
208
209
210
211
212
226
227
228
229
234
235
243
244
260
261
262
263
264
265
267
268
270
271
273
274
275
276

Suggested Trail Route ----- Other Trail ----- Unofficial Trail -+- Powerline === Dirt Road
Waterbody or Large River ——— Stream or Brook ——— Railroad ——— Paved Road •—• Gate P Parking Area
🔺 Peak, Summit, or Hill 3-Meter Contour

hundred feet to marker #201, then take a left. Briefly following an old gravel road, the wide trail gently rises and falls, passes beneath a large powerline, and in about 0.2 miles reaches a junction at marker #202. The RFT heads to the left, but go right and climb the steep western shoulder of Mt. Norwottuck on the M-M Trail for 0.3 miles via a series of switchbacks. At the top of the rise, stay left at a junction at marker #203. Continue to climb for 0.6 miles along the ridge to the summit of Mt. Norwottuck, at one point passing a spur path on the left to a scenic vista.

The partly open summit of Mt. Norwottuck offers broad views. From the top, the M-M Trail passes a short spur to an open ledge at the top of a high cliff, then descends steeply to the east for 0.2 miles to a junction at marker #205. Immediately after this junction, the trail descends through a narrow crack in the rock that requires some scrambling. Below is the area known as the Horse Caves (really more a series of overhanging ledges). The trail swings right, passes beneath the ledges, and continues descending eastward for 0.3 miles, along the way passing an unmarked junction with a rugged trail coming in from the left. At a junction with the RFT at marker #206, go right on the M-M Trail/RFT (they are concurrent here). Cross over a small knob, and in 0.2 miles reach a junction with the Ken Cuddeback Trail in another saddle at marker #207.

Climb steeply for 0.2 miles to a junction at marker #208. A worthwhile out-and-back spur path leads 0.1 miles north to a dramatic scenic vista at Rattlesnake Knob. From marker #208, drop steeply to the east and in 0.3 miles arrive at the top of Cliffside Trail in a flat area at marker #209.

Go left on Cliffside Trail, an old woods road that is washed out and a little bit rough in places. After ascending slightly for 0.1 miles, drop at a moderate grade for 0.4 miles to a junction at marker #274. Go left and traverse the north slope of Rattlesnake Knob for 0.3 miles to junction #265. Go left and, in fairly

Rattlesnake Knob in the Holyoke Range, as seen from Long Mountain.

rapid succession, go left at #264, right at #263, and straight at #262. Now heading west on the orange-blazed RFT, traverse the north side of Mt. Norwottuck, undulating gently along the slope for 0.8 miles to marker #261. Go left and climb briefly back to #202, then follow the combined M-M and RFT trails back out to The Notch.

NEARBY On the eastern side of the range, a challenging 3-mile loop can be made by taking the M-M Trail west from Harris Mountain Road up and over Long Mountain, then returning via an unnamed trail on the north side of the mountain.

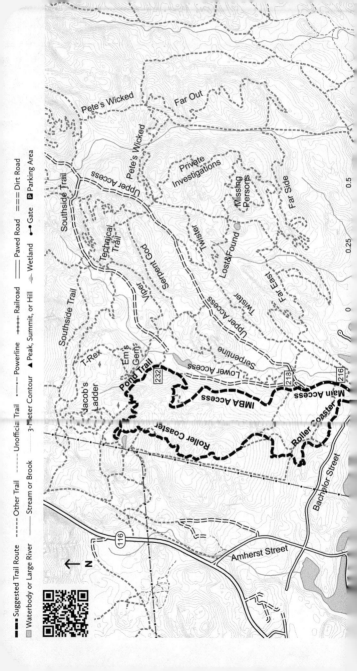

Legend

- ▪ Suggested Trail Route
- ▪▪ Waterbody or Large River
- ----- Other Trail
- ----- Unofficial Trail
- ▬▬ Stream or Brook
- — Powerline
- +++ Railroad
- ■ 3-meter Contour
- — Paved Road
- === Dirt Road
- •— Gate
- ⌇ Wetland
- ▲ Peak, Summit, or Hill
- P Parking Area

N

Pete's Wicked
Far Out
Pete's Wicked
Upper Access
Private Investigations
Southside Trail
Missing Persons
Far Side
Technical Trail
Serpent Good
Twister
Lost&Found
Far East
Southside Trail
Viper
Upper Access
Serpentine
T-Rex
Em's Gem
Lower Access
Jacob's Ladder
Pond Trail
232
IMBA Access
218
216
Roller Coaster
Main Access
Roller Coaster
Bachelor Street
116
Amherst Street

0   0.25   0.5

DISTANCE 3+ Miles **TOWN** Granby
DIFFICULTY RATING Moderate **TRAIL STYLE** Loop
TRAIL TYPE Singletrack/Doubletrack

A large portion of the southern slope of the eastern half of the Holyoke Range is laced with an incredible network of unmarked (though imaginatively named) singletrack trails. Compared to the Earls Trails network (see chapter 42), these trails tend to be more technical and challenging. Almost all of them require very careful navigation and route-finding. Few are blazed, and even fewer are marked with trail signs. Because the trails often meander so dramatically, it can be easy to lose your sense of direction. A GPS device might be particularly helpful for anyone checking the network out for the first time, and a detailed map is essential. Some of these trails were originally old jeep roads or hiking trails, but many were specifically built for and are maintained by mountain bikers. Although there is heavy use of these trails by mountain bikers, multiple uses are allowed and encouraged on all of them. The route described here follows one of the easiest and most navigable loops, though there are many junctions, and allowing extra time for getting turned around is advised for a first (or second) visit to the site.

DIRECTIONS From South Hadley, go north on Rte. 116 for 2.6 miles. Turn right and go 0.9 miles east on Aldrich Street. Turn left and go 0.2 miles north on Amherst Road. Turn right and go 0.6 miles east on Bachelor Street to the dirt parking area on the left, where there is space for about 20 vehicles.

TRAIL Starting at the parking area, take the yellow-blazed Main Access road north from the gate. As the name implies, this trail is the primary way into the Holyoke Range from the Bachelor Street parking area. It is a wide, mostly flat, doubletrack dirt road that runs north for about 0.3 miles. It heads straight into the woods and soon arrives at marker #216 where the double-track bottom of the original Roller Coaster trail leads left. Continuing straight, the road passes through a small open area and comes to a signed split where Main Access ends. The right fork leads to Upper Access, while Lower Access follows the left fork across a dip and past a junction—marked only by the rusty remains of an old vehicle—with the start of a narrower trail called International Mountain Bicycling Association (IMBA) Access.

At the junction marked by the junked-out vehicle (which comes just after crossing a small stream when heading north from the parking area), turn left and take the unblazed IMBA Access trail north. This 1.3-mile singletrack trail more or less parallels Lower Access most of the way, but it is longer and more interesting. With all its swoops and curves, it presents a slightly more challenging way into this part of the Bachelor Street network. Enter the woods and begin climbing the slope at a gentle grade. In a few hundred feet, bear right at an unmarked junction (the left fork leads up to Roller Coaster). About 0.5 miles along, the trail splits into two forks that rejoin again soon after. Take the left branch, which is slightly longer and curvier. Then begin descending the slope via long switchbacks to an unmarked junction with Lower Access trail just west of a beaver pond. Go straight, undulating up and down across the slope to a junction at marker #232.

Stay left on the Pond Trail and begin climbing the slope to the left at a steady, moderate grade. In 0.1 miles, pass an unmarked junction with a trail on the right. Continue straight and reach another junction at the top of a rise. Go left and climb via twists and turns to the top of Roller Coaster, just before reaching a powerline.

Roller Coaster is a 1.1-mile long trail that really does feel a lot like a roller coaster as it swoops and climbs and drops along a ridge. Heading south, it passes several short, unmarked spur paths leading right to the powerlines, and two faint, unmarked junctions with a now-discontinued branch on the left. Continue straight at all junctions. The trail soon splits into two branches that rejoin about 0.2 miles below; the right branch is more direct while the left branch meanders along the upper edge of a low ledge and passes an unmarked trail leading down to the left. The two branches rejoin at a junction near an old building foundation, where an overgrown road comes in on the left and creates a 5-way intersection. Stay straight on the singletrack Roller Coaster trail, which descends gradually, crosses a wide trail, and begins to swing left. It soon crosses another wide trail and then meanders east over a combination of rocks, roots, ledges, and soft pine needle mats back to the start.

NEARBY Other Bachelor Street trails are well worth exploring. Each has its own character and can be fun to run. Loops involving Jacob's Ladder, Serpent God, Lizard King, Far Side, Far Out, and Twister are all highly recommended.

DISTANCE 3+ Miles   **TOWN** Ware
DIFFICULTY RATING Moderate   **TRAIL STYLE** Loop
TRAIL TYPE Singletrack/Doubletrack

Quabbin Park, located on the southern shore of the Quabbin Reservoir between the towns of Belchertown and Ware, encompasses all of Quabbin Hill, a 1,026-ft. mountain that is laced with roads and trails. The route described here follows a mix of singletrack and doubletrack and includes deep woods, open meadows, a lookout tower, a scenic vista, and the water's edge. There are a few regulations: swimming is not allowed in Quabbin Reservoir, and vehicles need to be outside the gates by the posted time.

DIRECTIONS From Rte. 202 in Belchertown, go east on Rte. 9 for 6 miles to the eastern entrance for Quabbin Park. Go north on the paved park road for 2.5 miles to the sign for Hanks Meadow, then turn right and go a few hundred feet down the dirt driveway to the picnic area and parking lot.

TRAIL Starting at the Hanks Meadow parking area, go south on the dirt driveway and cross the paved park road. Pass Quabbin Gate 54 and go south on the old road (Old Webster Road), passing an elaborate foundation on the left at the start. Ascend very gently for 0.6 miles to a junction.

Optional Extension To add an extra 1.5 miles to your run, continue straight (south) on the old road. Pass a junction with a grassy road leading right in 0.4 miles. Several hundred feet farther, take the next right where the road forks. In 0.3 miles, turn right at the next

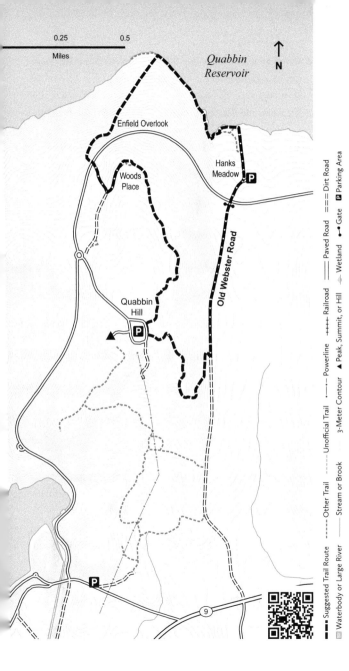

0.25   0.5

Miles

N

Quabbin Reservoir

Enfield Overlook

Hanks Meadow

Woods Place

P

Old Webster Road

Quabbin Hill

P

P

9

▪ Suggested Trail Route   ---- Other Trail   ----- Unofficial Trail   ------ Powerline   ++++ Railroad   === Dirt Road

Waterbody or Large River   —— Stream or Brook   —— Paved Road   ┴ Wetland   •— Gate   P Parking Area   3-Meter Contour   ▲ Peak, Summit, or Hill junction. Cross the powerline and bear left into the woods. The trail narrows and becomes a yellow-blazed singletrack trail here, and can be overgrown for the next mile or so. Climb the slope to the north, skirting to the right of a pond on a high bluff, then bearing left across the slope to a saddle on the southwest ridge of Quabbin Hill. Turn right here and follow the trail along the ridge. After a brief meander through some low scrub brush, you emerge at the south side of the Quabbin Tower at the top of the hill. Then resume the main route from the tower parking lot.

From the junction, go right on the yellow-blazed singletrack trail and gently climb the slope via a long switchback. It ascends steeply in places, with some intermittent sections of level grade, before emerging at the eastern end of the very large parking area for the Quabbin Tower. You will see the tower straight ahead across the lot.

Follow the edge of the parking area north for about 200 feet, then take the yellow-blazed trail right (northeast) back into the woods, just past a clearing. The trail meanders along the eastern side of the hill for about 0.25 miles until it reaches a glacial erratic boulder. Then it descends northwesterly at a gentle grade, passing through scenic fern glades with soft footing.

At a grassy clearing, the trail bends left, crosses an open area, then re-enters the woods along an old road. Soon it descends to a 3-way junction and turns right (the left fork would bring you up to a traffic circle in 0.25 miles). Descend the grassy road for 0.1 miles to the paved park road. The Enfield Lookout parking area is about 100 feet to the east.

Cross the road and follow the trail, now an old dirt road, as it curves to the right beneath the lookout's clearing. You then cross a small stream and follow the old road as it descends diagonally about 0.5 miles down the slope. The road ends at the southern edge of the reservoir. Here, take the yellow-blazed singletrack trail right (east) and pass through the edge of the woods about 10 feet up from the water. The footing is very good at first, with a surface of soft pine needles. In about 0.25 miles, the trail becomes a little rougher as it makes its way around several small rocky points and bays. Then it reaches and crosses a small stream and wet area. The trail then becomes somewhat difficult to follow, with some overgrown parts, unmarked splits, and confusing markings. All routes eventually lead back to the Hanks Meadow area, but to be safe stay as far left as possible, close to the edge of the water, until you come to a straight grassy old road. A left turn here will immediately take you to the edge of the water. Turn right and ascend at a gentle grade back to the parking area.

NEARBY About 8 miles southwest, a sizable network of unmarked singletrack trails winds through Facing Rock Wildlife Management Area in Ludlow.

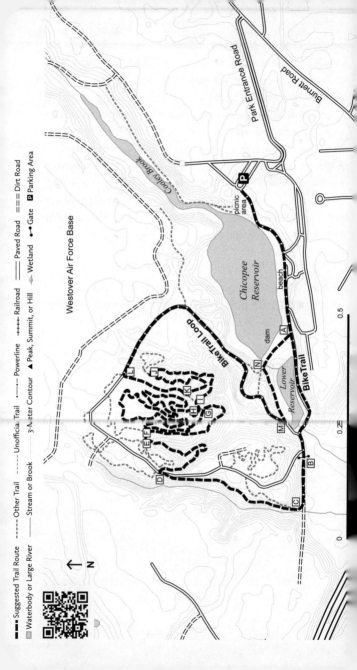

Westover Air Force Base

Cooter Brook

Chicopee Reservoir

Park Entrance Road

Burnett Road

picnic area

beach

dam

Lower Reservoir

Bike Trail Loop

Bike Trail

N

← N

- ▪ ▪ Suggested Trail Route
- ---- Other Trail
- ━━ Waterbody or Large River
- ----- Unofficial Trail
- •—• Powerline
- ——— Stream or Brook
- +++++ Railroad
- ——— Paved Road
- •—• Gate
- === Dirt Road
- ⌇ 3-Meter Contour
- ▲ Peak, Summit, or Hill
- 🅿 Parking Area

0   0.25   0.5

DISTANCE 4.5 Miles   **TOWN** Chicopee
DIFFICULTY RATING Easy/Moderate   **TRAIL STYLE** Lollipop Loop
TRAIL TYPE Singletrack/Doubletrack

Chicopee Memorial State Park is a narrow property located just north of the Massachusetts Turnpike (I-90) and just south of Westover Air Base. A paved bike path makes a lollipop loop on the western side, and a very dense network of singletrack trails has been constructed inside and around the paved loop. The trail run described here combines paved and unpaved sections of varying widths. It can be challenging to follow the exact route and it is easy to get turned around, but inside the loop you will never be far from the bike path. The suggested route can easily be changed up, and other trails can be added to increase the mileage.

DIRECTIONS From exit 6 off of I-90, take Burnett Street north for 0.6 miles. Turn left into the entrance for the park and go about 0.4 miles west to the parking area.

TRAIL From the parking area, follow the wide paved Bike Trail west 0.25 miles to the beach area at the upper reservoir. Continue west past both the bathrooms on the left and a trail leading north across the stretch of land and dam between the reservoirs on the right (map marker A), then descend a hill to the start of the Bike Trail Loop by the western end of Lower Reservoir at 0.6 miles. Go left and immediately arrive at a junction. Instead of going up the hill on the Bike Trail Loop, stay straight and pass through a metal gate (map marker B). Now on a level dirt road, go 0.1 miles west to a junction (map marker C). Take a right and, ignoring the steeper trail on the right with old metal railings, begin climbing gradually along the right side of a steep-sided creek on a trail that narrows to singletrack. In 0.3 miles you arrive at the paved Bike Trail Loop (map marker D).

Go left on the bike path for 100 feet, then take a sharp right onto a singletrack trail. In 50 feet, stay straight at a 3-way junction. Follow this meandering and undulating trail for 0.25 miles as it swings south down into a ravine and then north back up out. At a 3-way junction (map marker E), go right for 100 feet to another 3-way junction (map marker F). Go right again and make another 0.25-mile swing south and then north.

At the next 3-way junction (map marker G), take a left and follow the extremely twisting but mostly level trail for an entire mile to a junction (map marker H) just north of the one it leaves from. It nearly doubles back on itself many times but never once meets or crosses another trail. Go left at the junction, then right at the next junction in about 100 feet (map marker I). Follow the mostly level trail for 0.25 miles to a junction with the "stick" of a remote lollipop loop (map marker J). Go left and run 0.2 miles to a junction (map marker K). Then go right and follow a much straighter trail back out a junction with the paved Bike Trail Loop (map marker L).

Go right on the bike path and follow It southeast and then southwest for 0.6 miles. Just before it reaches the bottom of the hill and completes the loop, take a sharp left (at map marker M) and follow a dirt trail east to the dam between the upper and lower reservoirs (map marker N). Cross the dam back to the bike path, take a left, and return to the parking area.

NEARBY The narrower northeastern arm of the park features remote trails that will be more accessible once a bridge over Cooley Brook is replaced.

DISTANCE 4.5 Miles   **TOWN** Holyoke
DIFFICULTY RATING Challenging   **TRAIL STYLE** Loop
TRAIL TYPE Singletrack

A trail network on the western side of the Holyoke Community College (HCC) campus links up with the Metacomet-Monadnock (M-M) Trail along East Mountain just to the west. Some of the HCC trails appear to have been abandoned, but they can be followed with care, and occasional markers are still in place. The route described here uses some of these trails as well as the M-M Trail to form a roughly 4.5-mile loop. Note that the northern portion of this loop passes along an old road just south of an active shooting range; you may hear loud gunfire very nearby.

DIRECTIONS From exit 16 on I-91 in Holyoke, go west about 0.5 miles on Cherry Street/Rte. 202. Turn left and go south on George Frost Drive for 0.5 miles. Turn right on Campus Road and go about 0.1 miles to the visitor parking lot on the left.

TRAIL Starting at the parking area, go south along the paved road a few hundred feet past the campus police station to the trailhead on the right. The (occasionally) yellow-blazed trail climbs a low ridge. Follow it south, bearing left at a fork. Pass a junction with a trail on the left and descend to another junction, then bear right and descend to a stream. After crossing the stream on wooden boards, bear left at an unmarked junction and go a short distance to an old woods road. Go left on the road. Just before it crosses the stream, bear right on a different road. After crossing a wet area, the trail climbs steeply up a ridge, angling first to the right up the slope and then left. It levels out near the crest and eventually reaches a junction with the white-blazed M-M Trail. There is a very nice westward vista a short distance to the left (south).

Turn right on the M-M Trail and follow it north. It traverses the crest of the ridge for about 0.1 miles, then makes a sharp left to descend the west slope. It crosses a very jagged talus slope that requires careful attention to avoid rolling an ankle. Then it levels out and crosses a sandy road called the Trolley Trail. On the other side of the road, it climbs the slope to a 4-way intersection. Stay right on the M-M Trail and climb steeply to a ledge with a nice east-facing vista (an uncommon orientation for views along this ridge). Re-entering the woods, the trail continues north, rising and falling along the narrow ridge. It passes multiple ledges with views, traverses a few narrow fins of ridge, and eventually reaches an old beacon tower about 1 mile north of the Trolley Trail.

From the tower, the trail descends to the north. It passes a large boulder and then drops to a junction with an eroded old road in a saddle and bears left through a section with rough footing. Then it swings right again and climbs steeply to an open ledge with a very nice westward view. It then skirts along the upper edge of a cliff on the west side of the ridge. Near the northern tip of the ridge, the trail swings hard right and goes east about 0.1 miles over to the eastern side of the ridge. Then it swings hard left and descends steeply to the north. It passes tent platforms on the left and reaches Cherry Street Extension.

Go right on Cherry Street Extension for 0.5 miles. Pass two unmarked junctions with old roads on the right, either of which could be used as shorter alternate return routes, and climb slightly to a junction where the road swings left. Go right here and follow the trail south for 0.25 miles to a fork. Bear right at the fork and climb a short distance to the crest of this low ridge. You soon pass through an open area with views to the

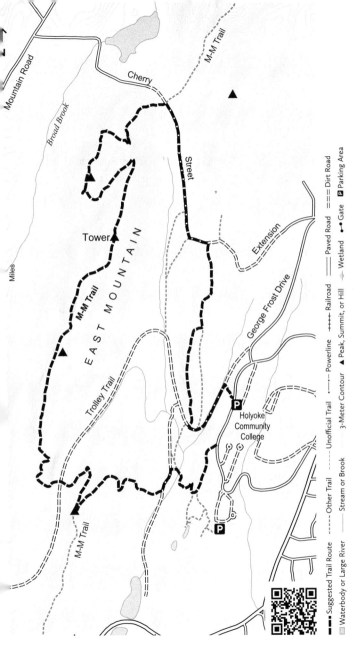

Mountain Road

Cherry

M-M Trail

Broad Brook

Street

Extension

Tower

George Frost Drive

M-M Trail

EAST MOUNTAIN

Miles

Trolley Trail

P Holyoke Community College

M-M Trail

P

Suggested Trail Route ----- Other Trail •—•— Powerline •••••• Unofficial Trail —— Paved Road === Dirt Road

Waterbody or Large River —— Stream or Brook ++++ Railroad ----- 3-Meter Contour ▲ Peak, Summit, or Hill •—• Gate P Parking Area ⋆ Wetland southwest. Descend south from here, following round blue trail markers down to a junction with Trolley Trail at some concrete blocks. Turn left on Trolley Trail and go 0.2 miles east to a junction. Turn right and follow the short trail up to the parking area.

NEARBY About 1 mile south of HCC, the 3.5-mile flat loop on dirt roads around Holyoke's Ashley Reservoir (where some sections on scenic causeways almost look like something out of J. R. R. Tolkien's Middle-earth), is perfect for beginner trail runners. A local running club hosts weekly cross-country races here in the summer.

DISTANCE 3 Miles   **TOWN** Westfield   **DIFFICULTY RATING** Easy
TRAIL STYLE Loop   **TRAIL TYPE** Singletrack

Just southwest of the wide-open fields of Stanley Park in West-field lies the mostly wooded Frank Stanley Beveridge Memorial Wildlife Sanctuary. The trail network here is popular as a racing site with local running clubs and cross-country teams, but it is also an excellent location for beginners looking for a gentle introduction to trail running. Although there are occasional rocks and roots, the trails are generally smooth, flat, and easy to follow. One note of caution: occasional dam releases at Cobble Mountain Reservoir upstream will flood several normally dry channels of the braided Munn Brook; anyone visiting the park should stay north of any flooded waterways.

DIRECTIONS From exit 3 off I-90, go south for 1.8 miles to the center of Westfield. Turn right on Court Street and go 0.8 miles west to where it becomes Western Avenue. Travel 1.3 miles west on Western Avenue. Turn left at the second entrance to Stanley Park and proceed 0.2 miles south to a parking area across from a playground. A map of the property is posted at the trailhead by the edge of the woods.

TRAIL Starting at the trailhead, go south on the red-blazed Access Trail. Drop down the slope at a moderate grade, passing a junction with another red-blazed trail from the parking area, to a T-junction with a dirt road below. Take a right and follow Access Trail west for about 0.3 miles, passing three junctions with narrow unnamed trails coming down the slope from the right, to a junction where the blue-blazed River Trail leads left.

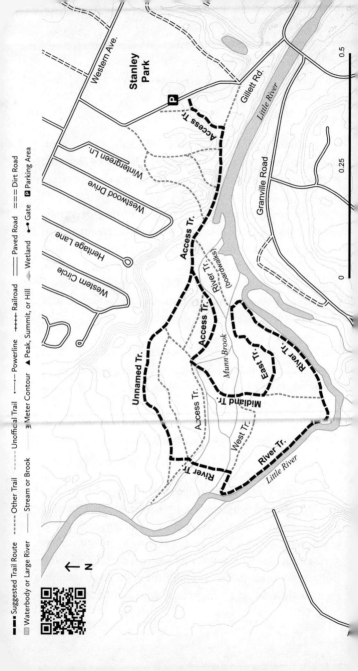

Stay straight on Access Trail. In about 0.1 miles, bear right on an unnamed and unblazed trail that passes to the right of an old orchard. At the far end of the open area, bear right at a 3-way junction and go about 0.3 miles west to a 4-way intersection. Turn left and go a short distance south to a 5-way junction.

From the junction, go south on the blue-blazed River Trail. In about 0.1 miles it crosses the normally dry, rocky channel of Munn Brook and then swings right (west), passing a junction with West Trail on the left. Soon the trail arrives at the edge of Little River where it swings left and follows the northern bank for about 0.6 miles to a junction with the yellow-blazed Midland Trail. Stay straight on River Trail for about 0.4 miles to a 3-way junction where River Trail crosses Munn Brook on a bridge.

Optional Trim to shorten your run, stay straight on River Trail and return to the red-blazed Access Trail, then turn right. This scenic route crosses a wetland on a long, wide boardwalk bridge and offers views of a riverside marsh.

Turn left at the bridge and follow the green-blazed East Trail west for about 0.4 miles to a 3-way junction. Turn right and go north for 0.2 miles on the yellow-blazed Midland Trail, passing the West Trail on the left, to a 3-way junction. Take a right and go about 0.5 miles east on the red-blazed Access Trail, along the way passing multiple junctions with trails on the left and one with River Trail on the right. Turn left at any of the junctions east of River Trail to return to the parking area.

NEARBY A few miles west up the hill from Westfield, the Appalachian Mountain Club's Noble View Outdoor Center in Russell features a dense network of trails that vary from easy to challenging. Highlights include well-maintained trails, plunging waterfalls, and a broad east-facing vista.

DISTANCE 3–4 Miles   **TOWN** Agawam
DIFFICULTY RATING Easy/Moderate   **TRAIL STYLE** Loop
TRAIL TYPE Singletrack/Doubletrack

Robinson State Park is a linear strip of land on the southern bank of the Westfield River in Agawam, encompassing forested terrace above, a steep bluff, and patches of floodplain forest below. It is more or less divided into east and west sections by a boundary pinch at the main entrance, with the western side being more developed with roads, picnic areas, and facilities. The entire property is laced with a network of meandering trails, especially the eastern side where the mountain bike trails are particularly dense. Most of the trails, especially the newer singletrack ones, flow well and contour organically across the landscape, though there are occasional eroded sections. Exposed roots are occasional throughout, but in general the trails here are very gentle and smooth, with remarkably few rocks. The New England Mountain Bike Association (NEMBA) has built bridges over many of the tributary brooks feeding into the Westfield River below, though there are occasional small stream crossings. Many trails are blazed, and it is possible to follow marked loops on the yellow, white, and red trails, but the markings are inconsistent and sometimes coincident, so be cautious about trying to use that system for navigation.

DIRECTIONS From exits 6 and 7 off I-91 in Springfield, take Rte. 147 west for 2.7 miles. Turn right on North Street and go west for 1 mile to the entrance for Robinson State Park on the right. Take the entrance road 0.1 miles north to the entrance. There is parking at a trailhead just to the right of the fee station. Three

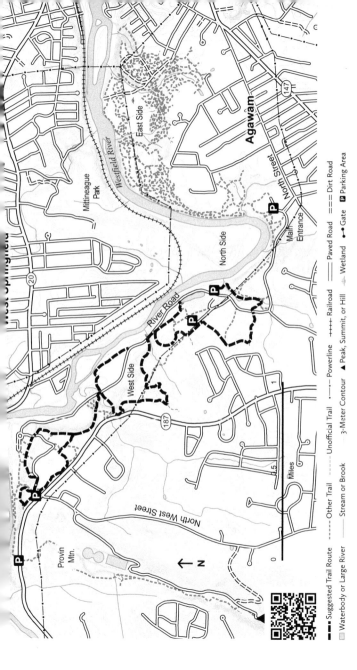

West Springfield

Westfield River

Mittineague Park

East Side

North Side

North Side

Agawam

North Street

Main Entrance

River Road

West Side

141

20

187

North West Street

Provin Mtn.

N →

Miles

0   .5   1

• ■ • Suggested Trail Route   ----- Other Trail   ----- Unofficial Trail   +++ Powerline   ═══ Paved Road   === Dirt Road

Waterbody or Large River   —— Stream or Brook   3-Meter Contour   ▲ Peak, Summit, or Hill   ⊷ Gate   P Parking Area   🟦 Wetland more parking areas are located near Robinson Pond about a mile to the west; to reach these, go left on the paved park road from the entrance and stay right at an intersection. It is also possible to enter the park at several gates along the southern edge of the property.

TRAIL This trail profile is unlike the others. Instead of providing turn-by-turn route guidance, which would be extremely difficult to either describe or follow, it offers brief synopses of the two halves of the park. A suggested route for the western side is provided on the map, but nearly any combination of trails on either side will make a fun run. Expect to get turned around (and maybe lost for a bit), especially if following the sinuous mountain bike trails that endlessly loop around and curve back on themselves.

The eastern side of the park contains one of the densest trail networks in the region. In addition to the blazed routes depicted on the park map, there are also countless narrow mountain bike trails that crisscross the main trails at unmarked junctions. The main trails tend to be straighter, more eroded, and rocky, while the mountain bike trails meander all over the place (on purpose, just for the fun of it) and tend to be smoother with better footing. If you choose to run on these trails, be alert for mountain bikers who could be coming from either direction, and courteously step off the trail to let them pass by.

The western side has fewer mountain bike trails and may be easier to navigate. There are a remarkable number of trails here, too. A paved park road, closed during the week, runs through the middle of it and can serve as a touchstone for navigation. The center of the park contains the lowest density of trails, though even at its narrowest pinch-point three separate trails parallel one another between the river and an adjacent neighborhood.

Optional Extension Provin Mountain. Although not shown on park maps, the Metacomet-Monadnock (M-M) Trail passes through the far western edge of the property. From the southern bank of the Westfield River, it heads west just above the riverbank for 0.25 miles, then rises steeply up the bluff to the terrace above. It then continues west and then south to a crossing of Rte. 187, where there is parking along the road. From here, it is possible to run approximately 3.2 miles south to Rte. 57 and back for a 6.4-mile out-and-back. The trail climbs up and over Provin Mountain, where there are several nice westward views of Westfield and Southwick from open ledges, and passes by an old quarry, a defunct TV station facility, and an observation tower.

NEARBY Along with a disjunct parcel of Robinson State Park, Mittineague Park in West Springfield lies just across the West-field River to the north, and Forest Park in Springfield is about 4 miles to the east; both sites feature networks of forested trails that are good for running.

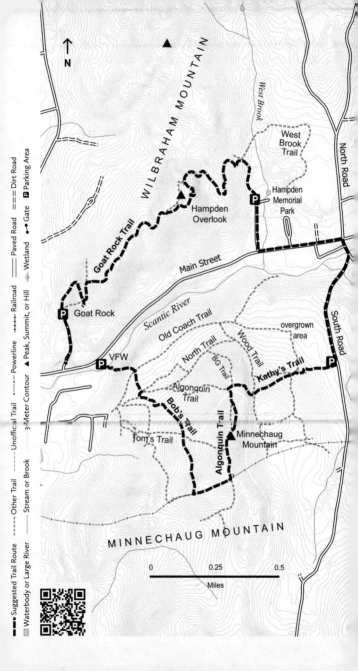

Map Legend

- ● ● Suggested Trail Route
- ━━━ Waterbody or Large River
- ------- Other Trail
- --------- Unofficial Trail
- ━━━━ 3-Meter Contour
- ━━━━ Stream or Brook
- ••••• Powerline
- +++++ Railroad
- ━━━ Paved Road
- === Dirt Road
- ≋ Wetland
- •—• Gate
- ▲ Peak, Summit, or Hill
- P Parking Area

↑ N

WILBRAHAM MOUNTAIN

West Brook

West Brook Trail

Hampden Memorial Park

North Road

Hampden Overlook

Goat Rock Trail

Main Street

P Goat Rock

Scantic River

Old Coach Trail

overgrown area

VFW P

North Trail

Wood Trail

Kathy's Trail

P

South Road

BG Trail

Algonquin Trail

Bob's Trail

Tom's Trail

Algonquin Trail

Minnechaug Mountain ▲

MINNECHAUG MOUNTAIN

0   0.25   0.5

Miles

DISTANCE 5 Miles **TOWN** Hampden
DIFFICULTY RATING Challenging
TRAIL STYLE Loop **TRAIL TYPE** Singletrack

A north-south line of forested hills rises abruptly to the east of the broad plain of the greater Springfield metropolitan area. Minnechaug Mountain supports a dense network of trails on conservation land, and the popular Goat Rock Trail traverses the southern end of the mountain just to the north. The loop run described here combines these two sites and includes about a mile of paved-road running in between.

DIRECTIONS From Somers Road in Hampden, go east on Main Street for 0.4 miles to the VFW parking lot on the right. If there is an event, alternate parking can be found at the top of Country Club Drive, at Hampden Memorial Park, and along South Road.

TRAIL Starting at the VFW parking lot, cross the Scantic River on a wooden bridge. On the south side of the river, the orange-blazed Algonquin Trail leads left up into the woods. Climbing somewhat steeply at first, it soon comes to a 4-way intersection with the Old Coach Trail. Continue straight on Algonquin to a second 4-way intersection in about 0.1 miles. Go right on the red-blazed Bob's Trail. In about 100 feet, go left at a fork and follow Bob's Trail upslope. The trail climbs more or less diagonally up the hillside at a moderate grade for about 0.4 miles to an easily missed 4-way intersection with the very steep white-blazed Tom's Trail.

Continue straight (south) on Bob's Trail, climbing gently for about 0.3 miles to an open utility line swath. Turn left (east) here and climb the grassy and rocky trail along the swath. It rises steeply at first, then levels out and arrives at a junction along the crest of the ridge. There is an eastward view straight ahead. Turn left (north) on the orange-blazed Algonquin Trail and climb gradually for about 0.1 miles to a junction with the upper end of Tom's Trail. Continue straight for a few hundred feet to the summit of Minnechaug Mountain, where there is a cleared view across the broad plain to the west.

Descend to the north from the summit on Algonquin. At a fork in the trail, stay right (the left fork rejoins about 0.1 miles below). At about 0.2 miles from the summit, go right on the blue-blazed Kathy's Trail at a junction. Pass the red-blazed Billy Goat Trail on the left and descend the eastern side of the mountain, first curving to the right and then left before arriving at a 4-way intersection. Go straight (east) on the unblazed trail, eventually passing junctions with an unmarked trail on the right and several trails on the left. Just before reaching an open field, bear left and rejoin the blue-blazed Kathy's Trail, then follow it down to a different open field. Trace the right side of the field, curve sharply left at the far end, and arrive at a small grassy parking area.

Go out to South Road and turn left. Be alert for fast-moving vehicles here. Run north down the hill for 0.5 miles to Main Street. Turn left on Main Street and follow sidewalks 0.35 miles west to the paved entrance road for Hampden Memorial Park. Turn right into the park. In 0.2 miles you will see a sign for Goat Rock Trail at the northwest corner of the parking lot.

Take the white-blazed Goat Rock Trail west up the hillside. There are many unblazed side trails and a junction with the western end of the blue-blazed West Brook Trail. Stay on the Goat Trail. It alternately climbs gradually via switchbacks and steeply straight up the hill. After passing through a flatter section of dense shrubs, the trail resumes climbing steeply and then reaches a junction where a blue-blazed alternate trail leads up to the summit. Stay left on the Goat Rock Trail. Soon you will come to two east-facing vistas over Hampden. From the vistas, follow the white blazes southwest along the ridge crest, passing the other end of the blue-blazed summit trail and several places where the trail forks. About 0.5 miles from the summit, you descend to a junction with a spur trail out to Goat Rock, an open ledge with a view southwest across the valley below. To descend, avoid the extremely steep white-blazes and instead follow the blue-blazed alternate trail down via a knee-saving switchback. You will come out at a cul-de-sac at the top of Country Club Drive. Go 0.2 miles down the road to Main Street and then go left for 0.15 miles back to the VFW parking area.

NEARBY There is a short but nice network of trails about 3 miles to the north along the Wilbraham Mountain ridge at Rice Nature Preserve in Wilbraham.

51 Peaked Mountain

DISTANCE 4.5 Miles **TOWN** Monson
DIFFICULTY RATING Peaked Mountain Tract—Moderate/Challenging;
Miller Forest Tract—Easy **TRAIL STYLE** Loop
TRAIL TYPE Singletrack/Doubletrack

Peaked Mountain, owned by The Trustees of Reservations (TTOR), lies along a north-south ridge between Hampden and Monson, just north of the Connecticut state line. While the actual summit is forested, there are numerous excellent views from ledges on both sides of the mountain. The property features a mix of old roads, hiking trails, and unmarked mountain bike trails. The route described here follows named trails only. A separate TTOR property, the Miller Forest Tract, lies a short distance to the north and also has a network of trails.

DIRECTIONS From Rte. 32 in Monson, take Ely Road 1.4 miles southwest. Merge onto Lower Hampden Road and go 1.9 miles. Turn left onto Butler Road and go 1.1 miles south to the gravel parking area for Peaked Mountain on the left. From North Road in Hampden, go 0.5 miles east on Main Street. Bear right at the Y-junction on Scantic Street and go 0.5 miles. Turn left on South Monson Road (which becomes Hampden Road) and go 2.5 miles east to Butler Road. Turn right onto Butler Road and go 1.1 miles south to the gravel parking area for Peaked Mountain on the left.

TRAIL Starting at the parking area, the trail heads east across the left edge of an open field behind the trailhead sign. Just after it enters the woods, bear right on the yellow-blazed Butternut Road trail at marker #1. Climb along this singletrack trail at an

204

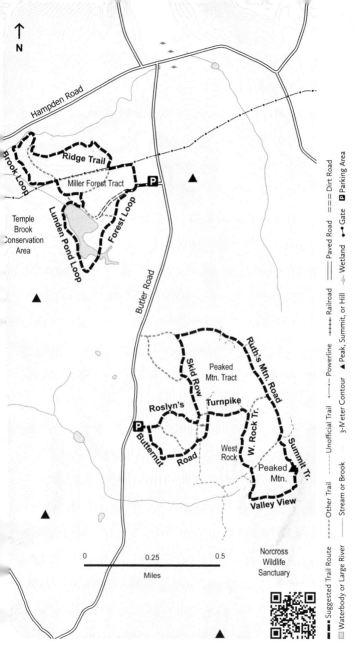

N

Hampden Road

Brook Loop

Ridge Trail

Miller Forest Tract

P

Temple Brook Conservation Area

Lunden Pond Loop

Forest Loop

Butler Road

Peaked Mtn. Tract

Skid Row

Ruth's Mtn. Road

Roslyn's

Turnpike

P

Butternut

Road

West Rock

W. Rock Tr.

Peaked Mtn.

Summit Tr.

Valley View

Norcross Wildlife Sanctuary

0   0.25   0.5

Miles

Suggested Trail Route · · · · Other Trail ----- Unofficial Trail · · · · Powerline ==== Paved Road === Dirt Road ••• Gate ▸• Gate **P** Parking Area

Waterbody or Large River —— Stream or Brook ·····• 3-Meter Contour ▲ Peak, Summit, or Hill ≋ Wetland easy grade to marker #2, then bear left and climb more steeply up to a junction at marker #3. Stay right and continue climbing to an unmarked junction with Dry Toes Bypass. Go right about 100 feet to another unmarked junction where an unnamed trail leads right. Go left here to an unmarked junction with Roslyn's Turnpike.

Turn right (east) and follow the red-blazed Roslyn's Turnpike, a wide and rough fire road, straight up the steep slope to a junction at marker #7, passing several unmarked junctions with mountain bike trails on the left. Turn right (south) on the red-blazed West Rock Trail and gently ascend to West Rock where there is a limited westward view. Descend slightly to a junction at marker #10. Continue south on the red-blazed Valley View Trail. In about 500 feet there is a far-reaching view west from an open ledge. The trail then swings east and passes an unmarked junction with a narrow, unblazed trail. Stay straight on Valley View and climb a short but steep, rugged slope to a ledge with an eastward view. The trail swings left and climbs a short distance to a larger ledge where there is an even better eastward view. The true summit lies a short distance to the west.

From the top, follow the red-blazed Summit Trail northward down to a junction at marker #9. Go right on the red-blazed Ruth's Mountain Road, passing several unmarked junctions with mountain bike trails on the right. At marker #8, stay straight on the now orange-blazed Ruth's Mountain Road and descend for about 0.5 miles northwest to a junction at marker #13. The descent is gradual at first, then steeper further down, and there are multiple intersections with unmarked mountain bike trails along the way. Turn left onto Skid Row (unblazed) and head south across the slope to a junction at marker #14. Turn left again, and climb slightly along the continuation of Skid Row (now orange-blazed) to a junction at marker #6. Turn right here on red-blazed Roslyn's Turnpike and follow it steeply back down past several junctions to the parking area. The loop at the main tract is 2.5 miles.

Optional Extension Go 0.5 miles north to the parking area for TTOR's Miller Forest Tract. A circuit loop along the outer trails utilizes a mix of singletrack and doubletrack and will add an extra 2 miles. From the parking area, follow the grassy road west to a junction at marker #16. Go left and keep taking lefts at the next two junctions. After crossing a short causeway over Lunden Pond, follow the trail around the south and west shores of the pond. At the north shore of the pond, stay straight at a junction where a trail leads left, then go left at the next junction. Go left at the top of the hill just past a cabin, then stay straight at the next junction. Staying left at the next three junctions brings you back to marker #16. The northern half of this loop descends along a small stream, climbs along Temple Brook, and passes through a wide variety of forest types, all on very runnable trails with only occasional short climbs and descents.

NEARBY Several miles south, across the Connecticut state line, Shenipsit State Forest is laced with great trail running possibilities, including 1,075-ft. Soapstone Mountain.